Venturing Into a Teenager's World

BY Richard D. Dobbins:

Your Spiritual and Emotional Power
Venturing Into a Child's World
Venturing Into a Teenager's World

Venturing Into a Teenager's World

Dr. Richard D. Dobbins

Fleming H. Revell Company
Old Tappan, New Jersey

Library of Congress Cataloging-in-Publication Data

Dobbins, Richard D.
　Venturing into a teenager's world.

　Bibliography: p.
　1. Adolescence.　2. Parenting.　3. Youth—Religious life.　I. Title.
HQ796.D55　1986　　305.2'35　　86-6462
ISBN 0-8007-1473-3

Copyright © 1986 by Richard D. Dobbins
Published by Fleming H. Revell Company
Old Tappan, New Jersey 07675
All Rights Reserved
Printed in the United States of America

Acknowledgments

———————◆———————

This book has been a family project. My children, Bill, Ilene, and Sharon, have contributed much to this manuscript. Without the experience of having lived through their teen years with them, I would have lacked a basis of compassion for understanding today's parents and teens. My wife has patiently read each chapter and has given me the benefit of her insights. My daughters have made me aware of the need to degenderize the material, and my older daughter, Ilene, has edited it.

Contents

———◆———

Part III: Helping Your Teens Take Control of Their Lives

Part IV: Helping Your Teens Choose Companions in Life

Part V: Helping Your Teens Develop Their Faith

Preface

Parenting teens in today's world can be an intimidating task. The moral risks for teens in our society are greater than they have ever been. Parental controls are being challenged as never before.

However, millions of parents and teens are making it through these difficult times together. So can you and your teens!

In *Venturing Into a Teenager's World* you will find the same emphasis on "good enough" parenting I stressed in *Venturing Into a Child's World*. Your teens don't require perfect parenting—just parenting that is good enough.

No parent can be perfect. Even if we could be, our children would not perceive us as perfect. However, with a little help, any parent can be good enough. This book is intended to help you reach that goal.

In the following twelve chapters, I have provided some useful information to help you discover how teens feel and think about their world as they prepare to enter adult life. I haved defined some biblical principles parents need to follow in launching teens into lives of their own. I have made some practical suggestions for implementing these principles in your relationships with your teens.

Remember, the kind of adults your teens become cannot be totally attributable to the kind of parent you are. Responsible parenting is important. However all of us have seen young people whose parents were negligent at best—perhaps even derelict—grow up to be men and women of excellent character and outstanding achievement. We have also seen young people raised by healthy Christian parents make disasters of their lives.

The choices that will shape your teens' futures belong to them. You are responsible for giving them opportunities to make good choices. However they are ultimately responsible for what they make of their lives.

It is my prayer that *Venturing Into a Teenager's World* will give you more confidence in your ability to provide "good enough" parenting for your teens and more courage to trust them with the choices necessary to discover God's best for their futures.

Introduction

———◆———

Usually sharing a similar experience builds understanding between people. However, having been a teenager doesn't seem to be of that much help to many parents when they face the challenge of parenting their own teens. Why? As parents, we tend to focus on how much more physically and morally threatening the world of today's youth has become, compared to the tamer days of *our* teens. Certainly few people would want to take exception to that fact.

Even though we grew up in a much more conventional day, we generated many of the same feelings in our parents that our teens are now generating in us. This fact is easy to forget.

Distance Between Generations Is Nothing New

Strained relations between parents and teens is as old as the human race. A careful look at Scripture indicates that there has always been a certain distance between generations.

Remember, Jacob couldn't get along with his father, Isaac. Absalom was a horrible grief to David. Both Samuel and Eli had trouble with their sons. These are just a few of many biblical examples.

This universal tendency for strained relations between parents and their young people is what makes Jesus' story of the prodigal son such a classic.

Bridges Are Built From Two Sides!

Bridging the distance that sometimes develops between parents and teens is a job both generations have to tackle. After all, bridges *are* built from two sides!

In the story of the prodigal son, both the father and the son had some hard work to do before the vast expanse of loneliness and rejection between them could be overcome. The father's love for his son had to become strong enough to support the son's search for himself. He had to love his son enough to let him go. And the son's love for his father had to grow strong enough to bring him home once he had found himself.

Notice the story carefully! Jesus didn't pronounce moral judgment on the father or the son. He didn't say the father was a failure. He didn't say the son was bad. He simply told their story: a story that's been repeated again and again throughout the history of the human family, a story that talks about distance that sometimes develops between generations and how love can bridge it.

Have Compassion for Your Teens

If you want to minimize the distance between you and your teens and the time required to bridge it, you'll work on becoming as compassionate as you can toward them. Practice putting yourself in your teenager's place. Imagine yourself growing up in today's world. After all, that is really what compassion is all about—caring enough to put yourself in another's shoes.

We have little difficulty understanding the need to show compassion for people who have never heard the gospel. We feel a tug at our hearts when we are confronted with the plight of those who are less fortunate than we. However the anxieties and frustrations of parenting often blind us to our teenagers' needs for compassion.

Compassion moved Jesus during His earthly ministry. Now, it motivates Him to intercede for us as our High Priest. His love for us enables Him to put Himself in our place. That is how He is touched with the feelings of our infirmities. He is able to put Himself in our place. He feels our struggles, our temptations. In compassion He reaches out to help us. The same Holy Spirit who gives Jesus the ability to be compassionate toward you will give you the ability to be compassionate with your teens.

Strange as it may seem, often showing compassion toward people we don't know is easier than reaching out to members of our own family. Incidentally, by sharing with your teens some of the struggles you have trying to balance love and discipline in your management of them, you can help them become more compassionate toward you.

Remember, the world of your teenagers is vastly different from the world in which you and I grew up. By reminding yourself of some of these differences you may be able to deepen your compassion for your teens.

The World Has Changed Since Our Teens

You see, since World War II, the normal distance between generations in our country and in many other countries of the world has been greatly widened. There are several factors involved in this change.

1. RAPID EXPANSION OF SCIENCE AND TECHNOLOGY. An explosion in scientific and technological advances has taken place—television; commercial aviation; atomic energy, with all of its complications; space travel; telecommunications; computers; automation of

industry. These are just a few of the things that you and I knew little about when we were growing up but are a part of the everyday world of today's teens.

Recently I became acutely aware of this scientific gap when I began to tackle the operation of a computer. Experts tell us that by the turn of the century people who are not computer literate will be as handicapped in our society as people who are verbally illiterate today. Since I certainly do not want to be a victim of this gap, I began learning how to operate a computer.

Accepting my grandson as my teacher was a very humbling experience for me. You see, computers are part of his normal school world. To discover that he knew so much about computers and I knew so little just underscored the tremendous difference between the world in which he is growing up and the world in which many of us grew up as teenagers.

The social changes resulting from this scientific and technological revolution are hard to imagine. The distance between the agricultural world in which our parents and grandparents grew up and the industrial world of our teen years is very small compared to that between the world of our teen years and the computerized technological space age in which our teens are growing up.

2. MATERIALISM HAS TAKEN OVER. Today's emphasis on materialism is greater than ever. Commercialism in modern America is rampant. By many, things are considered more important than people. A person's value is blatantly equated with what he or she owns.

The Christian knows this flies in the face of everything Jesus teaches. In Luke 12:15 He cautions His disciples about this danger, "Take heed, and beware of covetousness: for a man's life consisteth not in the abundance of things which he possesseth." Nevertheless, modern Americans believe otherwise. We are caught up in unparalleled materialism.

A famous evangelist was invited to be the house guest of a wealthy Western rancher. Before they sat down to dinner, the rancher wanted to impress the evangelist with his wealth. So the two of them walked out on the west side of a veranda, which continued around all four sides of the house.

The rancher pointed to the west, where oil rigs were pumping as far as they could see. "They're mine," he said. "As far as you can see. They're mine."

Then the two of them walked around to the south side of the veranda. There the rancher pointed out over wheat fields, bending low with a promising bumper crop. "They're mine, too," he said. "As far as you can see. They're mine."

Proceeding around to the east, the rancher pointed to a forest of virgin timber, which extended as far as they could see. "It's all mine, too," he reported.

Just before they reentered the house, they strolled around to the north. There the rancher proudly pointed to a huge herd of thoroughbred cattle grazing on the plains, which stretched toward the distant horizon as far as they could see. "And they're all mine, too," he said, hoping to impress his guest.

Refusing to be taken in by this deceptive display of opulence, the evangelist pointed upward toward the sky and asked his host, "How much do you own in this direction?"

Feeling the sting of the spiritual challenge, the rancher bowed his head and admitted, "I guess I've neglected that."

People are more important than things! Our world measures people's worth in terms of what they own. The Word of God tries to help us understand how deceptive this measurement is by focusing on the transient nature of things.

So raise your teenager in an environment where people are obviously more important than things. After all, man was not made for riches—he was made for relationships. Paul reminds Timothy of that in 1 Timothy 6:7, "For we brought nothing into this world, and it is certain we can carry nothing out."

Sometimes in emphasizing the futility of materialism, I will quote that passage this way: "We brought *no thing* into this world, and it is certain we can carry *no thing* out."

But what is it that we *did not* bring into the world with us that we *can* take out? Our relationships—with God, our parents, our children, our brothers and sisters, and our brothers and sisters in Christ.

Riches stay here, but we can take our relationships with us when we leave. They are like treasures stored up in heaven, where moth and rust cannot corrupt or thieves break through and steal. Your teens need to be very aware that your relationships are more important to you than your riches.

If you want your children to observe these priorities in their lives, be sure you set the example. You must be careful to avoid being caught in the trap of materialism yourself if you want them to learn how to escape it. Remember, your children will tend to do what you do, *not* what you say.

3. MOBILITY HAS FRACTURED EXTENDED FAMILIES. Few young people in today's America have the luxury of growing up around their extended families. On the other hand, when we were growing up, some of us lived close enough to our grandparents to know them well and enjoy their love. Our uncles and aunts lived nearby. We went to school with our cousins. We enjoyed the luxury of being part of a larger family group.

With so many family members in our daily world watching what we did and listening to what we said, we tended to lead a somewhat more disciplined life than people in today's world. Since all around us were people who knew us and knew our families, we cared about what they thought of us, and we didn't want word of any misbehavior to get back to our family.

The dawn of the "nuclear family." However, when the parents of today's teens were growing up, this kind of extended family began to break down. Following World War II, couples began to leave their families to find jobs in other parts of the country. We became a nation on the move. Today, 50 percent of the families in the United States move every five years. Finding teenagers who have been raised around their grandparents, their uncles, their aunts, and who find some of their closest friends among their cousins is unusual. Even coming across teenagers who expect to graduate from high school with friends who started to go to first grade with them is unusual.

This new kind of American family, consisting of parents and their children living hundreds of miles apart from the rest of their families, draws its name from the dawning of the atomic age, which spawned it. Sociologists have dubbed it the "nuclear family."

Our cities and metropolitan areas have become vast seas of anonymity, created by floods of nuclear families driven together by their frantic search for employment and prosperity. Such an environment is hostile to healthy marriages and strong families. When we're surrounded by people who don't know us and care little about what we do, moral erosion spreads rapidly. Marriage becomes one of its first victims.

4. DIVORCE IS SHATTERING THE NUCLEAR FAMILY! Divorce is at near record levels in the United States. Most of the parents of today's teens grew up in unbroken nuclear families—headed by their natural parents. Security and identity were much more easily established in such a sheltered environment than in the highly unstable single-parent and reconstituted families of today.

Many in this generation of teens not only lack the benefits of the extended family, but also see their own nuclear family shattered by divorce. Almost 50 percent of today's first-time marriages end in divorce. Three-fourths of these divorces occur before a couple reaches thirty years of age, right at the peak of the child-bearing years of a marriage. As a result, almost half our nation's children are being deprived of the security of growing up under the care of both their natural parents. Therefore, in addition to the normal developmental struggles, they will face the greater complications of being raised in homes broken by divorce. This makes a big difference in the world of today's teens.

When most of us parents were growing up, we didn't experience having to become acquainted with mom's boyfriends and dad's girl friends. Today many teens find these experiences a part of their everyday world.

If you have been crushed and hurt by divorce, you know how

devastating this pain is. Unfortunately, sometimes divorced parents become so preoccupied with their own pain that they are unaware of what their children experience as they helplessly watch their family break up.

Remember, if you are divorced, your teens have gone through the divorce with you. Let me suggest that you reach out in a vulnerable moment to allow them to open up and share their feelings with you. Let them know you are touched by their pain and that you are also hurting. This sharing will help you to be compassionate toward each other. "Bear ye one another's burdens, and so fulfil the law of Christ" (Galatians 6:2).

5. NO ONE IS YOUNG FOREVER! The unhealthy way we currently segregate our generations also tends to distort the world of today's teens. We put our babies and preschoolers in day-care centers. Younger boys and girls go to elementary schools. Grandparents, if they are around at all, are often in a rest home somewhere else in the community.

So unlike the world in which you and I grew up, where we were often around babies and old people, today's teens live in a much more highly segregated subculture of their own. They are seldom around babies, and they avoid older people. Teenagers do not want to be reminded that someday they will be old and wrinkled. Many teens want to escape into a fantasy world of faddish hairstyles, fashion clothes, and video music. They want to be teenagers forever. How realistic is that?

Helping them come to terms with the reality that faces them requires us to build some bridges into their world. Of course, they must do some bridge building, too. If we are to keep our relationships intact and move through the future together, then both generations have their work cut out for them.

Adolescence Gives Parents Another Chance

The first section of this book acquaints you with ways you can help your teen develop his or her personality. You will see the personality of your child change dramatically during adolescence. The extent of this change becomes obvious when you meet a young person you haven't seen since childhood. He or she is like a different person.

The other day I met a young man I had not seen since he was in first or second grade. He is now as big as I am. I was struck with how capable and intelligent he was. When I last saw him, imagining him as a teenager carrying on such a conversation with me would have been difficult, if not impossible. I remember the concerns his parents had for him. He had had some severe clashes with school authorities, but no discernible trace of those problems was evident in my conversation with him. He was in college and doing well. Somewhere, in the process of growing up, he worked out those issues with his parents and teachers.

One of the wonderful things about adolescence is that it gives you a chance to correct some mistakes you may have made in the early years of your parenting.

The child's whole personality seems to open up in early adolescence. These years give you a tremendous opportunity to get into the teens' world. Become vulnerable to them, and invite your teens to open up to you. Some of the things you were not able to build into the early years of their lives you can add in now.

SOMETIMES PARENTS MUST FACE CRISES WITH TEENS. Unfortunately, adolescence is not always a happy time for young people. Many of us know teens who were delightful and happy-hearted children. Yet between childhood and adulthood their world caved in on them.

The other day I sat with a sixteen-year-old who is pregnant. There are no good choices for sixteen-year-old pregnant girls. They are too young to marry. When marriage is attempted, it very often fails. If the young lady is a Christian, she is certainly not going to have an abortion. If she keeps the baby and does not marry, she will seriously limit the baby's world and her own. On the other hand, a sixteen-year-old has extreme difficulty considering parting with a baby and adopting it out to some other couple. The fact that the couple are Christians may alleviate the struggle to some extent, but it certainly does not eliminate it. Sixteen years of age is too early in life for any young woman to be faced with these kinds of decisions. But they have to be made.

The Three Stages of Adolescence

Teens pass through three generally identifiable stages of adolescence:

1. *Early adolescence—from years twelve through fourteen.*
2. *Middle adolescence—from years fifteen through seventeen.*
3. *Late adolescence—from years eighteen through the early twenties.*

During this journey your role as a parent will become more and more that of a guide and confidant. Your teens will make more and more of the choices that will shape their futures. However your prayerful supervision and loving guidance are essential if your teens are to build wholesome futures. The five sections of this book provide some global tasks your teens will need your help in accomplishing. The chapters zero in on specific tasks within each of these areas.

Developing Personality

Your teens will need your help in developing their personalities, and we will be taking a journey into the rapidly changing physical world of young teens. You will see why learning to feel good about their bodies is such a big challenge for young men and women. Early adolescents are growing more rapidly than most any other thing you see in nature. Coordinating all of that growth while continuing to feel good about themselves is a major task.

Then of course, once a young man or woman is comfortable with his or her new adult-sized body, he or she begins to notice members of the opposite sex. We'll see why Adam and Eve was a great idea as young men finally discover young women and young women are relieved to find they are not going to be ignored forever.

In late adolescence separation from the family usually occurs. Young people begin to discover the ways they and their families are alike and the ways they are different.

Stewardship of the Body and Mind

Next we will look at your role in helping your teens take good care of their bodies and minds. The two big fears parents have are that their children will damage their minds with drugs or become involved in a premarital pregnancy. Both of these issues are addressed very plainly. I will help you know when teenagers may be experimenting with drugs and what you can do about it. Then we'll have a frank discussion about sex from a biblical point of view and consider some practical suggestions for discussing this vital subject with your teens. Since less than 30 percent of teenagers can talk about sex comfortably with their parents, accepting this challenge will put you in a highly distinguished minority.

It Is Time for Your Teen to Take Control

Years ago when those little cuddly, warm bundles of love came into your home, you knew you had about eighteen years to prepare them to take control of their lives, but you never dreamed time would pass so rapidly. Well, it has, and now your teens need your help in assuming responsible control of their own lives.

Understanding that everyone has someone to tell them what to do is difficult for adolescents. They have been "bossed" by their parents for so many years. They just assume that when they get to be adults they will have outgrown their need for a boss. It is shocking for them to discover that as long as we live someone, or some group of persons, will be in authority over us.

GOD'S LOVING AUTHORITY IS GOOD FOR US. God wants us to discover that healthy limits on our behavior are good for us. That's one lesson that came through loud and clear in the Garden of Eden. The earlier in life we can learn this, the less of our potential will be wasted. Your teens face the challenge of learning to define their own healthy moral boundaries. As children, these decisions were largely made for them by their parents and their church. Now they must learn to make them on their own.

DIRECTION FOR THE FUTURE. Facing the future successfully requires more than defining healthy moral boundaries. You have to have a job. Discovering and developing their vocational gifts is another big challenge for teens.

By the time a young person is out of high school he or she should have acquired some saleable skill. Teens need to consider their Christian career choice. How early should it begin? How can you help your teens see that vocational choice should come before mate choice in their priorities? These and other questions will be explored.

IN CASE OF REBELLION. Parents' fear of rebellion in their teenagers is very common. When it occurs, rebellion is usually encouraged by poorly chosen friends, and poorly chosen friends are usually the result of a negative self-image. By helping your children grow up with good feelings about themselves, you have gone a long way toward preventing teenage rebellion.

In fact, statistics tell us that only 20 percent of our teens take the rebellious route toward the future. Take a look at your family. Realize the likelihood is minimal that you are going to run into serious difficulty with any of your teens. The risk is even less if you get acquainted with their world and learn some of the bridge-building skills suggested in this book.

However, for those who may be faced with the challenge of managing a rebellious teenager, suggestions are given for shortening the period of rebellion and lessening its pain. A plan is presented for peacefully separating an older adolescent from the family when his or her life-style is too different from the family's for either to tolerate. A temporary separation is much more desirable than the continuation of such a very destructive war.

Parents and Peers

Your teens will need help in choosing the other important people in their lives. Friendships and—eventually—mate choice will form an extremely important part of your teens' futures. From early adolescence to adulthood, your teens will move farther from their family and closer to their peers. Teens need to know how to choose their friends wisely and how to build healthy friendships. I will show you how to help them develop some practical skills for doing this.

IT IS NOT GOOD FOR MAN TO BE ALONE. Only your teens' choices of their faith and vocation are more important than the choice of a mate. I explain our American mate selection system and the role biblical principles should play in it. Some important reasons are given for taking a serious look at the family from which a boyfriend or girl friend may come.

Helping Your Teens Develop Their Faith

You and your teens can come to a better understanding of the process by which young people discover and develop their faith. We will talk about ways you may be of help to them, but the struggle is theirs. Remember that! Don't try to wage it for them. They must determine what their faith will be—what they want to believe.

ENCOURAGING SPIRITUAL GROWTH. When we come to know Christ, we are spiritual infants. In fact, Jesus refers to the beginning of our spiritual life as a new birth. If we follow the developmental model suggested by the new birth, we should expect a new convert to grow from infancy to childhood to adolescence to maturity in his or her faith.

As you can see, young people are poised for great spiritual growth, but they need to discover the difference between a supernatural faith and one that is magical or superstitious. Remember, the supernatural is neither magical nor superstitious. Learn how to demonstrate the differences so your teens can make this important distinction.

How beautiful it is when spiritual growth comes from the inspiration of a teen's father and mother. One of the most satisfying experiences of parenthood is to help your teens into deeper spiritual discoveries.

Youth pastors and pastors frequently have this joy; however the inspiration for this part of life's journey is much more appropriate coming from you, the mom and dad of the teenagers. Life has few more rewarding experiences than observing your teens' efforts to obtain the spiritual potential that God has placed within their reach.

Now that you have had a glimpse of where we are going, let us begin venturing into a teenager's world.

Part I

Helping Your Teens Develop Their Personalities

One

Feeling Good About Me

———◆———

Years ago I was speaking for a pastor whose children were in their teens. During the morning worship service, some misbehavior occurred in the area of the sanctuary where the pastor's thirteen-year-old boy was seated. I'd seen the whole incident. I knew that the youngster was innocent. However, when we got into the family car and started out for lunch, the pastor angrily proceeded to chew out his thirteen-year-old son right in front of the rest of his family and my wife and me.

I tried to defend the youngster without directly confronting the pastor, but he resented even the hint of my defense. He got angry. His face flushed as he said, "Sooner or later you'll discover that you can't believe a thing a kid says."

Refusing to forsake the young man in his innocence, I said, "You can if you've trained him well."

Trust Your Teens

The parents of teens need to responsibly supervise them and exhibit trust in them at the same time. This is not as paradoxical as it sounds. For example, in this case I've just referred to, if either of the boy's parents had been watching carefully, their son's innocence would have been obvious, and they would have trusted his report of the incident.

As adults, you and I like to be trusted. We don't like to be mistrusted because of someone else's irresponsibility or punished for someone else's misbehavior. Our teens don't like it either!

It is important that your teens know you trust them. They also need for you to believe in them. Your approval is a major source of their self-esteem. Be sure you keep it within their reach.

When they do a good job, tell them. Be as quick to praise them when they do well as you are to correct them when they do wrong. Don't require perfection! Remember, improvement deserves encouragement. If they know they have your confidence, they are more likely to try harder to keep it.

In helping your early teens develop their personalities, your major task will be generating good feelings in them about themselves. Your sons will need encouragement in becoming masculine, and your daughters will need to be helped in becoming feminine.

You will be less mystified by your teens' behavior and more likely to understand it if you remember that early adolescents, from years twelve through fourteen, are preoccupied with rapid physical growth, roller-coaster moods, and role identity. This chapter suggests some ways to help your teens feel better about themselves in this physically and socially awkward time of their lives.

Rapid Physical Growth

The age at which the adolescent growth spurt occurs varies widely. For a majority of boys it occurs between their ninth and sixteenth year. For girls, it is more likely to occur before their fourteenth year. The timing of this outburst of growth and the way your teens choose to respond to it can be important factors in the development of their personalities.

The schedule of our physical growth is determined by a part of the brain called the hypothalamus. As it matures it stimulates hormonal activity, resulting in a tremendous growth spurt in early adolescence. The hypothalamus also coordinates that growth.

The head, the hands, and the feet will reach adult size first; then the legs and the arms start to grow. Once they start, you wonder if they will ever stop.

Your sons will outgrow their trousers long before they outgrow their jackets. In fact, in one year, early adolescent males may grow from four to six inches. The change is not nearly so dramatic for females. However they often grow from one to three inches in one year.

Every Inch Has to Be Fed!

Parents soon become aware that every inch of this growth has to be fed. Some close friends of ours have raised three sons. They were amazed at the rate of their growth in early adolescence. Sometimes those boys would grow six inches a year! The shortest one now is six feet two inches; the tallest one is six feet eight inches. When the tallest was fourteen, he was six feet two inches.

When you realize that all these inches of arms and legs are acquired in a year or two, you begin to understand why young people are attracted to music with such a strong, rhythmic beat.

Later we will talk more about the moral issues raised by the lyrics of that music. However, it should be easy for parents to understand why the style is so appealing. The beat helps early teens coordinate all the new inches of arms and legs that they are growing, and the volume gives them a place to escape.

Awkwardness Is Normal

Learning to live in a body that is becoming so strange and different is awkward. One of the minor tragedies of early adolescence is that young ladies develop intense interest in young men about two years before young men even seem to be aware that young ladies exist. This adds to the awkwardness!

During this time young ladies may be very interested in the latest popular form of dance. However, boys won't develop a similar interest for a couple of years. Nevertheless the surging sexual interests of teens do not need this kind of additional unnecessary sexual excitement.

Remember how self-conscious you were during this time ? I can. Males' shoulders were broadening. Our hips were narrowing. We were getting facial and body hair, but we wished we could grow more—and faster! Our vocal chords were lengthening. When we opened our mouths to talk we didn't know whether we were going to sound like a tenor or a bass. This time in life is very, very awkward for young men.

Young women are also very self-conscious. They are beginning to menstruate. Their hips are rounding out. Their waists are narrowing. Their breasts are beginning to develop. It is obvious from the way they dress that, at times, they don't know whether to try to hide what is happening to them—or overadvertise the fact.

From the body of a child is emerging the body of an adult. In this "tween-age time," when youth are too old to be children and too young to be adults, they need patience from their parents.

Teens become very sensitive about these physical changes, so be careful not to tease them. Fathers tend to be more guilty of this than mothers. Dad, take it easy on your teenagers. What may seem to you to be a joke is a hostile or embarrassing attack as far as your teens are concerned. Don't tease them or make fun of them yourself, and don't permit their brothers and sisters to tease them either. Help your teens to accept these physical changes as the beginning of a very exciting time in their lives.

Early growth for the girl places her in the awkward position of being taller than all her peers—males and females. Similarly, the later developing boy feels just as conspicuous about being the shortest among his peers.

BREAKAGE RATES GO UP! During this time of rapid physical growth, expect things to be broken in your home. That way you won't be disappointed. Remember, early teens seldom walk into a room. They often stumble in. Rather than sit on a chair, they wrap themselves around it. Adolescence is an awkward time!

Perhaps you could generate more compassion for your teens if you could imagine yourself on stilts. All of a sudden you find yourself with four to six more inches of height and with two to four more inches of arms. How gracefully do you think you could walk? How efficiently do you think you could handle things? You and I have been the same height and had the same reach for so long that we easily forget we were once just as awkward as our teens.

Puberty

The word *puberty* comes from the Latin word *pubertas*. It means "age of manhood." Puberty marks the onset of a young person's capability of biologically parenting children. Of course, more subtle changes in sexual maturation begin much earlier. However, the presence of pubic hair reveals the potential to reproduce in both your sons and your daughters.

For girls, this age will vary from nine to fourteen. That means, of course, that before your daughter menstruates she should know about ovulation, menstruation, and reproduction. Although you can depend on the public school to generally inform her about these life processes, her ability to talk with you about them is very important.

If you need to rehearse the facts for yourself before talking to your daughter, your pediatrician will be glad to supply you with a booklet that will explain them to you. Since, during their teens, sexual concerns will be a major preoccupation of your youngsters, developing the ability to talk comfortably with them about this subject is essential.

Boys reach the age of puberty somewhere between ten and a half and sixteen. Celebrate your son's entrance to manhood. In fact, learn to celebrate each new event with your teens. When your sons get to be close to six feet tall, congratulate them on their growth.

When your daughters begin to menstruate, let that be an occasion for the family to celebrate their entrance into womanhood.

Roller-Coaster Moods

Of course, in addition to rapid physical growth, your early teens are coming to terms with roller-coaster moods. They are introduced to adolescence by a biochemical explosion that shatters the calm of their childhood. Hormonal activity goes on a rampage. Once those little time bombs start going off in their bodies, life for them begins to change in a hurry. They move from late childhood into adolescence like a flower bursting into bloom. Life will never be the same for them again.

This transition is accompanied by a gradual increase in aggressive and sexual energies. Early adolescents are extremely driven. All of this additional energy must now be integrated into a useful, socially acceptable life.

It's Normal to Be Abnormal!

This is one time in life when it is normal to be abnormal. When you know the tremendous chemical changes which are taking place in adolescents, you can understand why teens are so tense and touchy.

Holding these feelings in check all of the time is difficult. In fact, that is why the years from twelve to fourteen are often referred to as the time of tears and tantrums. You never know when your young person is going to burst out in tears or break out into a tantrum.

Remember, early adolescence is a time of normal abnormality. When I explain this to parents who are parenting their first teen, they seem to grasp it. Often, however, just a few moments later they will protest, "I just don't understand it. I know all you have said is true, but our child has never acted this way before."

Then I reassure them again, "That's right. Your child has never behaved this way before. When this transition to adulthood is over, your child will never behave this way again. Compared to the way he or she behaved as a child and the way he or she will behave as an adult, his or her behavior now is abnormal. However, your son or daughter is not a child anymore and it will be several years before he or she will be an adult. So, you can't compare your teen with either. When compared with what's going on in every other early adolescent, the way you say your son or daughter is behaving is perfectly normal and healthy." Being able to believe this somewhat alleviates parental anxiety.

Overreacting is a rule of life for early adolescents. One time you can say something to your teens, and they will take it very well. However, on another occasion you can say what you believe is the same thing, and they react very differently. This unpredictable nature of their moods is a major source of anxiety and frustration for parents.

For apparently no reason at all your teens may rush off in a huff or retreat into mysterious moods that no one understands—not even the teens. To ask them to explain what they are feeling and why they are feeling that way is foolish. They are simply growing through a phase.

Mothers who are going through menopause while they are parenting teens have a built-in base of compassion. You know how strange the hormonal activity in your body makes you feel from time to time. You don't know whether the temperature in the room is too warm or if it's just you. Like your teens, your moods will fluctuate on a similar kind of roller coaster. You can readily understand that just as the decrease of hormonal activity affects the moods of the woman in menopause, the increase of hormonal activity affects the moods of your early teens.

Testy Years Between Parents and Teens

This is the time when your teens may begin to withdraw from you. You should be alert for early signs of rebellion. In a later chapter, I will have more to say about how these can be detected and ways they can be managed. However, only 20 percent of our teens go through adolescent rebellion, so relax!

The thirteenth and fourteenth years are usually the roughest for a mother-daughter relationship. All of a sudden, the sweet little girl of yesteryear seemingly has become her mother's enemy, and open hostility erupts between them.

If you, as a mother, can remember the time when you became a young woman, you may be able to recall that you and your mother went through a similar struggle. After all, when a young woman develops her secondary sex characteristics, she has the figure of an adult woman. And—she wants her mother to know that she is just as much a woman as her mother is. At times she insists on being treated like a woman, but at other times she wants to be treated like a child. No mother can perfectly anticipate such rapidly changing expectations.

Daughters may become sassy and frequently challenge Mother's authority. If the mother doesn't overreact, daughters will usually outgrow this in a year or two. However during these months the teen's likely to be mouthy, competitive, aggressive, and hostile toward her mother.

Whenever necessary, Dad needs to step in to defend Mother. Often he can furnish the stabilizing influence that will help both mother and daughter manage their relationship much more constructively. He should insist that his daughter respect her mother. If he thinks his wife has dealt unfairly with their daughter, he should privately talk to her about it. A wise couple never allows the management of teens to divide them.

However, if the father has built a good relationship with his daughter, he should know that she is very much in love with him. If he will give her some fatherly attention, take some time with her, and show her some affection—hugging her from the side and kissing her on the cheek—he can take some of the heat off the mother-daughter relationship, help the mother manage the daughter better, and make it possible for the daughter to experience a smoother transition from girlhood to womanhood.

The most difficult years for the father-son relationship are usually the fifteenth and sixteenth. Many sons are larger than their fathers by this time. If the son's respect for his father has been rooted more in fear of him than in love for him, he may begin to test his father's authority over him. Even when a strong bond of love between father and son exists, some testing of Dad's limits may be expected.

THEY ARE TOO BIG TO SPANK. Your teens are acquiring physical dimensions that make it obvious that you can't control them by the fear of corporal punishment anymore—even though in desperation you may think of it at times. Of course, in most families children haven't been spanked since they started going to elementary school. Nevertheless, the obvious physical superiority of the parents enabled them to continue securely controlling their children.

Early adolescence brings an end to this kind of control. As children become physically as large or larger than their parents it often triggers off some very frightening feelings of powerlessness in parents. Your children are too old to spank and yet not old enough to behave as wisely as you would like them to behave.

Be patient with them. Think of how patient God is with you when you don't call all the right shots in your life. Let your guidance shift more from external controls that you have imposed upon them in the past to internal controls that you have helped them build through the years.

Remember, they are just beginning to assume the direction of their own lives. They will make mistakes; but if you have loved them and disciplined them in love, believe in what you have taught them. After all, you have been their model.

Trust what you've invested in your teenager. In most cases, you will discover you have done a far better job than you think you have. As you relax your authority a little, you will be relieved to see your teens beginning to build some controls of their own into their lives.

Role Identity

Early adolescence is the time when young men and women learn to be comfortable with their society's gender roles. The way they feel about their bodies and the relationship they have with their fathers are the two most important factors in developing a healthy gender identity. How your son feels about his masculinity and how your daughter feels about her femininity should be clearly discernible by the time they enter senior high school.

Teens Are Preoccupied With Their Bodies

Young teens have a strong preoccupation with their own bodies. They are extremely anxious about being too different from others. A male is concerned about his height, his physique, his facial and body hair, and the size of his penis. He wants to be as tall as other males. He wants his shoulders to be as broad as his peers'. He wants to shave as soon as his beard grows. And he wants his penis to be just as big as others he sees in the locker room.

EARLY AND LATE GROWTH CAN POSE PROBLEMS FOR MALES. Of course, young men who experience their physical growth early have a distinct advantage over their peers. Often they become leaders. However, there are also some definite disadvantages. For example, other adults, including their parents, expect them to behave as if they were as old as they look.

Earlier I referred to a fourteen-year-old boy who was six feet two inches tall. When he would goof off and act like any normal fourteen-year-old boy, his mother would become very impatient with him. I had to remind her, "He may have the body of a man, but he is still just fourteen years of age."

If your son gets his physical growth early, you will need to continually remind yourself that regardless of how grown-up his body may look, his brain has only been here since his birthday. It is not fair to expect him to be more mature than his years in his behavior.

Sometimes, when a boy is late in getting his growth he develops crippling feelings of inferiority and self-consciousness. This is understandable. After all, even though he eventually finds himself as tall as most of his peers, he has been the shortest in the group for a long time.

If your son is in this position, becoming anxious with him is not going to help him. A trip to the pediatrician can be very reassuring. There he will discover that the timing of his growth is genetically determined. If it is a little slow in coming, he doesn't need to worry. Most pediatricians prefer not to use growth hormones to stimulate growth. Except in rare cases, it is not necessary. Sometimes where hormones are used to allay the teen's anxiety, more immediate growth is gained at the sacrifice of some of the youngster's ultimate growth potential. Being patient and letting nature take its course is usually wiser.

Perhaps the best news you could give a young man in this situation comes from studies that indicate those whose growth spurts occur later in adolescence eventually tend to be taller than those who get their growth earlier.[1] So, if he can be patient, his peers may have been taller than he for two or three years, but he is likely to be taller than they for the rest of their lives.

The Role of the Father in Gender Identity

In helping your sons develop healthy personalities, remember the importance of their feeling good about being masculine. Having a muscular body, developing athletic prowess, being able to compete, becoming an achiever, belonging to the group—these are important aspects of being masculine in our society. The way your teenage son feels about himself is likely to be affected by his reaction to these cultural expectancies.

One of the most important factors in determining how masculine boys become is found in the boy's relationship with his father. Highly masculine boys tend to have fathers who are nurturant, but dominant and decisive in setting limits and administering both rewards and punishments to their sons.

Your daughters, of course, are concerned about being feminine. They are very particular about their clothes, their cosmetics, their hair, their shapes, and their breasts. They don't want their breasts to be either too small or too large. If their breasts are too small, they feel inferior about them. If they are too large, they feel conspicuous.

Being feminine in our culture does mean being attractive to men, but not for the wrong reasons.

Believe it or not, more feminine mothers do not raise more feminine daughters. The daughter's relationship with her father plays the critical role in the development of her femininity.

A daughter's viewing her father as being masculine is very important. If he wants feminine daughters, a father must reward them for acting feminine and participating in feminine events. His approval of his wife as a model for their daughters also seems to play a critical role in encouraging a daughter's femininity.[2]

Social Identity

Teens Want to Be Like Their Peers

Early adolescents find it extremely important to be like other teens—they don't want to be thought of as different. They want to be as tall as, as neat as, as well dressed as anyone else in their group. So they have a very strong need to be like others. Something as simple as a pimple on the face may become a major catastrophe. Parents need to minimize these problems for their teens as much as they can.

If your son or daughter develops a severe case of acne, a visit to a good dermatologist becomes a must. Otherwise you run the risk of skin problems also becoming emotional problems because of their effect on the way your teens see themselves. Since most cases of acne can be controlled, if not completely cured, why compound the issue? Problem complexions are much more easily treated than troubled emotions!

Dental care and eye care are also very important during these years. Our oldest daughter had very poor vision. We got her contact lenses as soon as the optometrist was willing to prescribe them for her, but that was not until she was sixteen. So during these early teen years, even though we tried to make the frames as cosmetically attractive as possible, she had to wear glasses with ghastly thick lenses. When she could lay aside those thick-lensed glasses and face the world with contact lenses, there was a dramatic difference in the way she saw herself.

THE PEER GROUP BECOMES MORE IMPORTANT. In early adolescence, the peer group becomes more important than the family as a source of self-esteem. This is why your family's involvement in a church with an active youth ministry is extremely important. Your teens need healthy peers.

CHURCH AND SCHOOL ARE VERY IMPORTANT! So many times I see parents who choose a church to suit their own needs. The wise parents of adolescents will find a church their teens also like. Friends are extremely important to teens. The peers your teens choose during these critical years can make or break their futures. The friends they find in church are much more likely to be healthy and wholesome than those they meet in public school.

Youth ministry is an attempt on the church's part to provide a wholesome peer group for teens and to bridge the distance between teens and their parents. As a parent, you need all the help you can get. In a healthy church with a good youth ministry, you have another professional person who is trying to keep the distance minimized between you and your young teens.

If the public-school environment is too destructive and the family is financially able to afford it, consider sending your teens to a private Christian school. In making this decision, it is important that your teens see it as a desirable option. Forcing them to go to a church-related school seldom does any good. However, frequently when the opportunity is presented in a positive way it is very attractive to them.

Consider the Moral Issues

YOU CAN'T ELIMINATE MORAL RISKS, BUT YOU CAN LIMIT THEM. Where the public-school environment is destructive and your teens do not want to go to a Christian school, consider moving to a less objectionable public-school district. These can often be identified by inquiring about the premarital pregnancy rate and the number of substance-abuse offenses recorded in your community's public-school districts.

Often, parents are critical of their teens' school friends but fail to realize the effect their neighborhood environment has on these choices. If you have chosen to live in an undesirable neighborhood, how can your teens make desirable friends?

When we were parenting our teens, we lived in a very lovely area that boasted an academically superior school system, but the substance abuse and premarital pregnancy rates were very high; so I found a district where both of these rates were considerably lower. We moved there. That move did not eliminate these risks for our teens, but it certainly lowered them considerably.

SEXUAL INTEREST PEAKS IN THE TEEN YEARS. Teens have a very strong preoccupation with sex. They think about it much of the time. Their sexual feelings are coming alive. Not since their pre-school days has sex been so prominent in their thoughts and their fantasies. They are experiencing the strongest sexual urges of their lives.

Although at times talking with your teens may be awkward for you and them, compassionate parents will want to help their teens manage their sexual feelings constructively and bring them under the lordship of Christ. Giving teens guidance in learning how to feel comfortable with their new sexuality is critical. This kind of help should come from the home and the family.

WHAT IF YOU CATCH YOUR TEEN MASTURBATING? During early or middle adolescence is when you are most likely to discover your teen masturbating. This is a very awkward moment for both of you.

Parents, fearing this moment, have often asked me, "What should I do?" My standard answer is, "When you are faced with the situation, don't overreact! Don't condone the practice, but don't condemn it either. Give them the same respect you would want them to give you if they came into your bedroom unannounced when you and your mate were making love. You would probably want them to back out and pretend they didn't see what they saw. So why not do the same for them? Then, later, in a more composed moment, you

will need to talk to them about their sexuality and masturbation."
Suggestions for this approach will be made in chapter five.

How the parent manages a situation like this leaves a lasting impression on the young person. I have sat with many, many people who point back to the traumatic time when, as teens, they were angrily confronted by their parent in such a moment. No doubt their parents loved them very much; however, good parental intentions don't keep those hostile, impulsively chosen words from haunting a young person's feelings about himself or herself. Being talked to in a condescending and demeaning way at such a vulnerable moment can become a major psychological trauma for a young person.

Role Models

Healthy adult role models are essential in helping young teens feel comfortable in their gender roles. Usually these will come from outside the family. This is a critical need for males raised by mothers in single-parent families.

Whenever a healthy relationship with the boy's natural father is available to him, it should be encouraged. When this is not a possibility, the single mother is sometimes able to encourage a relationship between her son and his grandfathers or uncles and other healthy males in the church.

Your young teens will begin to show a marked increase in emotional and intellectual abilities. These need to be challenged. Provide your teens with opportunities to learn and broaden their interests. Encourage their involvement in athletic activities. This will help to keep their mounting aggressive and sexual energies directed into constructive channels.

Middle adolescence has a new set of challenges for the developing personalities of young people. In the next chapter, I will provide some practical suggestions for helping your teens make the most of them.

Two

Adam and Eve
Was a Great Idea

One of the minor tragedies of adolescence is that young women become intensely interested in young men about two years before young men know young women exist. In the middle teen years, fifteen to seventeen, young men make this discovery. When they do, they agree—Adam and Eve was a great idea!

In middle adolescence, young people are easier to get along with than they were when they were in their early teens. Notice, I said that it's eas*ier* to get along with them—but it still is *not* easy.

In the middle teen's world, the preoccupation is with other guys and gals, getting out of the family, and God.

Other Guys and Gals

First, let's zero in on the social life of the middle teen. In those years from fifteen to seventeen, young people want to be on the go all the time. This means the family's communication and transportation resources are going to be pressed to the limit. In fact, you can count on a shortage of family telephones and automobiles. I will have more to say about regulating these things in chapter six, "Coming to Terms with Authority." During this time, responsible parents are going to become very concerned about the friends and social environment of their teenagers.

Know Your Community's Teenage Hangouts!

Make it your business to know the teen hangouts in your community. These are usually places where young people can gather in groups to talk, listen to music, and dance. In your survey, don't overlook the fact that the traffic in drugs can be heavy at some rock record shops. Take the necessary time to inform yourself about what goes on in these places. Don't take your teen's word for it. Find out for yourself!

I'm not implying that your teenagers would purposely deceive you. (Although I do think many of us can remember when, as teens, we thought it might be in our best interest to keep our parents in the dark about certain things.) I'm merely suggesting that teens are going to see things from a teen's point of view. However, they don't have the experience you have to help them measure the moral risks in their social environment. That's why they *need* your perspective. They may not *want* it, but they *need* it.

So by all means learn to know the teenage hangouts of your community and determine for yourself which are safe and which are not safe for your son or daughter.

SUGGESTIVE DANCING. In some of these places you are going to find suggestive dancing is featured. When you bring this subject up for discussion with your son or your daughter, be prepared for an argument. They are likely to say, "What's wrong with the way we dance? You're just trying to find fault. You don't understand. We don't even touch each other when we dance. What can be wrong with dancing like that?"

Then you can agree, "Yes, I've noticed that you don't touch each other when you dance." Go ahead and point out to them that even though dancing of that kind doesn't involve touching, it fires up the fantasy by involving motions that simulate sexual intercourse. Explain to them that this often means the touching, or attempts to touch, will come later.

Even though, on the surface, your teens may heatedly disagree with you, underneath they will respect you because it is obvious that you know what you're talking about. If they still want to argue, then make a date with them to watch one of the popular TV dance shows or video music programs. As you are watching it with them, point out the motions you're talking about and ask them what these motions are supposed to suggest. When you confront them with the evidence and make your case, I think you'll find it will help them open their eyes to some things that their own teenage biases keep hidden from them.

BEWARE OF DRUGS. In many teenage hangouts a very free-and-easy environment exists. Often, drugs can be bought easily there. In fact, if you have a nose for marijuana, when you go into some of these places, you get a whiff of the sickening sweet odor of its smoke.

In some teenage hangouts, alcohol is sold. It can't be sold legally to teenagers; but if you're in touch with their world, you know how easily an ID can be faked. Frequently, unscrupulous adults are also willing to help teens get alcohol.

Your teenagers need to know that for them alcohol is just as illegal as any other drug. In fact, it is the drug that poses the greatest risk for today's teenager. I'll be talking to you more about this in chapter four, "It's Dumb to Blow Your Mind."

If you discover the place where your teens want to hang out poses any of the threats we have been talking about, present your evidence calmly and convincingly. Then firmly make the place off limits for them. However, if you find the place your teens want to hang out with their friends is well supervised by responsible adults, free from drugs, and really does provide a wholesome environment for young people, by all means give your permission for them to go there. People who provide such places deserve the success your support will help them achieve.

KNOW THE HOMES OF YOUR TEENS' FRIENDS! Become acquainted with the parents of your teens' friends. You may be thinking, *But all my teens' friends are Christians. When my son and daughter visit their friends, they are in the homes of Christian parents.* That's good. However, most of us are not in the church very long before we find that some Christian parents are very careless with their teens. You need to know the risks parents are willing to take with their teens before you assume your young people are safe with them.

For example, how long do these parents leave their teens alone and unsupervised? Many Christian parents are naive enough to believe it is perfectly safe for them to go away and leave young people at home alone and unsupervised for hours.

Finding parents who care as much about their teenagers as you do about yours—and are just as careful in supervising them—is very reassuring. You can feel safe when your teens are in their home. They can feel safe when their teens are at yours. After all, the safest environment for middle teens is in their own home—or in the homes of friends their parents trust.

TRUST YOUR TEENS—BUT SUPERVISE THEM ANYWAY! Teenagers need their privacy. When our children were growing up, we tried to acknowledge this need by keeping a recreation room in the base-ment, furnished with music that we approved of, games, a game table, and some old furniture we didn't mind being roughed up.

When our teenagers brought young people home with them, we gave them the privacy of the basement. However, we were aware that there is no substitute for the responsible adult supervision of teenagers.

So every five or ten minutes we'd open the door to listen to what was going on. About every fifteen minutes or half hour we'd take down a fresh supply of cold drinks and popcorn. This way we were able to provide privacy for them and the inconspicuous supervision they needed was also maintained. That's the least parents can do to limit the risks of today's very threatening social environment for their teens.

Other Safe Places

Your church also provides a trusted place for young people. Try to locate in a church that has a good, active youth ministry. We talked about that earlier. Of course, its spiritual emphasis is of primary importance, but an active social program is also a must. Such a church will usually sponsor several wholesome events for your young people each month.

Sometimes school-sponsored events may be safe places for your teens. However, the moral realities of today's public schools require the responsible parent to investigate adequately before assuming this. Much will depend on the location of the school district. Even more important is the personal morality of the principal and your teen's teachers. After all, these are the people who will be making decisions about which activities will be permitted and how closely they will be supervised.

If you get an uneasy feeling about the moral environment of the school or the kind of supervision your youngsters would have in school-sponsored events, then you will want to limit your teens' participation.

The social safety of Christian schools is another plus for Christian parents to consider when deciding where their children should be educated. A Christian school will never adequately compensate for the lack of spiritual priorites in the home. However, if you are disciplined in your pursuit of wholesome spiritual priorities in your home, making the sacrifice to send your children to a school that embraces similar values can be a very wise investment in their futures.

In fact, the moral threat of public junior-high schools and high schools in many of our large metropolitan areas is so great that I frequently advise parents to send their teens to Christian schools if at all possible. In rural areas and smaller communities the risk is less, but even in these places the responsible parent will want to know those to whom he is entrusting his youngsters during these critical years of character formation.

Guys Eventually Discover Gals!

In their middle teens, your guys will finally discover gals. Typically, your gals have seriously doubted that day would ever come. Believe me, once it arrives, they are ready for it.

So during the middle teens, it's not unusual for a guy and a gal to fall madly in love, carry on a very intense relationship, and break it off completely—all in the same week.

In an attempt to keep young people from being hurt so deeply when such a relationship breaks, parents sometimes make fun of it. They may refer to it jokingly as "puppy love." Don't do that! This kidding only adds to your teens' pain and infuriates them with you. It becomes just one more bit of evidence to convince them you don't understand. Remember, to the "puppy," that love is very, very real.

The big discovery involved in the middle teens' first "love" relationship is that they are now capable of developing very deep, intense feelings for a person of the opposite sex. Such an experience is normal and healthy. Draw this to your young persons' attention. It's an indication they feel sufficiently loved and secure to risk this kind of intense and intimate involvement. However, they should not emotionally overinvest in this first relationship.

Help them realize that they probably will be in and out of many relationships before they eventually settle down to one person for a long period of time. Even though getting into and out of relationships like this hurts, something very positive is happening to your teens during this process. They are learning a set of social skills that will help them form a relationship, properly manage its physical limits, and emotionally survive withdrawing from it.

Developing these skills by getting into and out of short-term relationships creates confidence in their own desirability and furnishes them with an important tool for a healthy approach to mate selection. We'll be talking more about this in chapter ten, "Mate Selection—Chance or Choice!"

Telephone Courtships Lead to "Touching" Times!

During the early part of the middle teens, much of the lovemaking will take place over the telephone—that's a safe place for it to occur. As yet the young man doesn't have the ability to drive, but he has the desire to talk to the girl who has caught his fancy. So the two of them will talk on the phone.

At times *talk* may not be the word to use to describe what they are doing. They may just listen to each other breathe over the phone. The convenience of this mechanical bridge allows them to create some intimacy without the risks that a physical contact with each other might mean at this time. Parents should take comfort in knowing that it is physically safe for their teens to be close and intimate on the telephone.

The skill teens develop in telephone conversation helps them overcome their social awkwardness. Later, when their relationships are carried on more personally, they will have greater confidence in their ability to maintain them.

Once guys and gals begin to pair off in high school friendships, they want to express their affection physically—they want to kiss and neck. Sometimes parents exaggerate the threat this brings. I'm not saying you should ignore it. Certainly you should caution your young people about keeping their activities above the shoulders. Also stress the importance of limiting this dimension of their dating experiences to a few minutes. When these limits are observed, the kissing and necking that go on during middle teens is not so much an expression of deep and intimate love as it is the novelty of exploring a new world—experimentation with a new experience.

Stewardship of the Body

As your teens become young men and young women, they should know what the Bible has to say about our stewardship of the body. Paul says it very clearly and very plainly in 1 Corinthians 6:13–20:

Now the body is not for fornication, but for the Lord; and the Lord for the body. And God hath both raised up the Lord, and will also raise up us by his own power. Know ye not that your bodies are the members of Christ? shall I then take the members of Christ, and make them the members of an harlot? God forbid. What? Know ye not that he which is joined to an harlot is one body? for two, saith he, shall be one flesh. But he that is joined unto the Lord is one spirit. Flee fornication. Every sin that a man doeth is without the body; but he that committeth fornication sinneth against his own body. What? know ye not that your body is the temple of the Holy Ghost which is in you, which ye have of God, and ye are not your own? For ye are bought with a price: therefore, glorify God in your body, and in your spirit, which are God's.

In this passage Paul plainly teaches that the body of the believer belongs to God and to his or her mate. Sexual intercourse is designed by God to symbolically celebrate the union of two people in marriage. Until a person is married, he or she is to avoid such intimate physical contact with anyone. This discipline over the body will keep life free from the complications of sexual misbehavior.

THE GIRL SETS THE LIMITS! In launching her dating life, your teenage daughter needs to be lovingly reminded that girls get pregnant—not boys. Each year, this happens to at least 1 million teenage girls in our society.[3] What a sobering fact!

In seminar discussion times I'm often asked why the responsibility for setting the limits of physical contact in a dating relationship rests with the girl. Although the moral standards are the same for both sexes, two biological facts dictate my answer. First, teenage young men experience much stronger hormonally induced sexual urges than teenage young women. This makes the guys less conscious of the needs for limits at the time when they are required. Second, teenage young women get pregnant.

Morally, Christian young men are just as responsible for the stewardship of their bodies as are Christian young women. However young women are better prepared biochemically to be the limit setters, and their risks are much higher if the relationship gets out of bounds.[4]

As unfair as it may seem for nature to thrust such a responsibility onto young women, this is a fact that is not likely to change. Furthermore, parents who are raising daughters need to face this reality squarely, so they can help their daughters to come to terms with it.

For these very practical reasons, your teenage daughter will need to assume the responsibility for controlling the amount of physical contact she permits in her friendships with boys. She needs to understand that Christian guys are still males, and even though their faith should make them more amenable to the Scriptures, they are experiencing the same strong hormonal stimulation that makes every other guy aware of aggressive sexual energies during his middle teens. In fact, at about eighteen, the sexual urge in males reaches its peak. A guy will never be more "turned on" than he is during his late teens and early twenties. Your daughter needs to know that.

When a young man is sexually excited, his penis becomes erect. Teach your daughter to be alert for the protrusion that will occur beneath his clothing and to know what it means. If she becomes aware of his excitement while they are embracing, this should be an indication to her that she needs to cool things down. She can do this by changing her position and putting some space between them. A change of conversational topics also helps. Without offending or embarrassing her boyfriend, she can stay in control of the relationship. This will help both of them end their time together feeling better about themselves and each other.

BEWARE OF BODY SNATCHERS! Some young women are extremely fearful that their boyfriends will reject them. In therapy I've had young women say, "If I don't let my boyfriend have the liberty he wants with me, he won't go with me anymore. He'll start seeing someone else."

Help your daughter learn to detect where a young man's interests are very early in her relationship with him. If he is only interested in her body, she needs to realize that. After all, there are many other bodies out there in his world. If he is only interested in a physical relationship, let him find one with someone who has similar interests.

However, if he's really interested in her and he's a Christian, helping him keep their physical affection within the bounds of their Christian consciences will not discourage his attention. In fact, her limits will raise his respect for her, and his fascination with her is likely to deepen.

Explain to your daughter that the more the physical activity of a relationship is kept above the shoulders, the easier it is to control. This information should come from you—her parents. After all, who knows the wisdom of this information better than you? You've been through all this. You can look back on those times when you wish you had come home a half hour sooner—when things went a little further than you liked. Perhaps not all the way, but too far for comfort. So don't let your daughter go through this period of her life as unprepared for it as you were. Teach her the need to stay in control of these situations.

CHRISTIAN YOUNG MEN ALSO HAVE CONSCIENCES. Most Christian young men also have very active consciences in this regard. They want to control their behavior. They may need some help from their girl friends, but they feel better about themselves when they respect the bounds Scripture sets for their behavior. They know intercourse belongs in marriage, and they want to respect that fact.

Teach your son the sexual risks a young woman assumes in dating. Help him understand the wisdom of keeping his relationships free from the concerns that inevitably result from being sexually active outside of marriage. I will be more specific about these in chapter five "Looking Forward to Marriage."

Be sure your son understands that only when a fellow is financially capable of supporting a wife and has provided her with the emotional security of marriage does he have the right to expect her to go "all the way" with him. Until then, having intercourse with any young woman is irresponsible.

ENCOURAGE A VARIETY OF DATING PARTNERS. Wise parents are going to encourage their teens to have a variety of dating partners. I never will understand why some parents encourage their teenagers to go steady. Any mature adult who has had plenty of experience in observing teens will tell you that the physical dimension of a boy-girl relationship is much easier to control when a young man has several girl friends and a young woman has several boyfriends. This experience is also an important asset in the mate-selection process, which we'll be examining in chapter ten, "Mate Selection—Chance or Choice!"

Getting Out of the Family

Young people in their middle teens experience a very strong urge to get away from the family. So often, during this time, they think that parents would keep them in the family forever if they could. I try to relieve them of that fear when I talk at youth conventions. I assure them, "Hey, don't think you're the only ones who will be glad when you leave home. That will be a relief for your parents, too. If they have a good marriage, they've been looking forward for years to the time when they can lay aside the responsibilities of parenthood and enjoy each other more."

Only about 20 percent of our nation's teenagers find it necessary to rebel against their parents in order to get out of the family. But if your teenager is going to rebel, this is the time it is most likely to happen—in the middle teens. However don't mistake normal expressions of independence for rebellion.

The kind of rebellion I'm referring to involves very destructive social behavior: the destruction of property, sexual misbehavior, stealing, blatant profanity. These are the kinds of hostile expressions that announce that you have a rebel on your hands.

Once you see these signs, you know you are going to need professional help for the family. I would suggest that you talk to your pastor. He will probably be able to put you in touch with a professional person in the community who can take an objective view of your situation and help you and your teen manage it in the least destructive way. Possibly a person on the staff of your church is trained and skilled in doing this.

I'll be giving some more specific help with this kind of situation in chapter eight, "Getting the Best of Rebellion."

PLAYING SECOND FIDDLE TO PEERS AND THEIR PARENTS. When young people step out of their own family, they are looking for surrogate parents. These are often found among the parents of their friends or other adults who have earned their respect through the years.

Temporarily, your teens may turn to people like this and be closer to them than they are to you. By all means, don't be jealous of your teens' relationships with their friends' parents. Don't think that any other adult is going to take your place permanently.

Often, while your teens are turning to other adults, you will become a surrogate parent for some of their friends. These kinds of transitional relationships are particularly healthy when they can be formed within the church.

Many parents are shocked when they discover the extent to which the peer group replaces the family during these midteen years. It is hard for them to believe that teens would actually choose peer values in preference to those of the family.

This is the time when teens may become involved in some kind of substance abuse—drinking or blowing some grass. By all means, don't panic if this happens. In most instances you will be dealing with experimentation, which is usually brief and fleeting. This kind of behavior is often resorted to impulsively by teenagers as a way to relieve some of the anxiety they feel during this awkward transition from childhood to adulthood. Your young person should come through this relatively unscathed. Substance abuse is dealt with in greater detail in chapter four, "It's Dumb to Blow Your Mind."

Temporarily, these peer relationships are very important in the life of your teens. However, parents need to understand how brief and transient these relationships are. For example, can you name four or five of the teenagers you were close to during your middle teens? I can't. I'll venture to say that you can't either. What makes you think your teenager will be any different?

Right now their peers are very important to them. But if you don't panic, these relationships will fade away in the next five years or so. Your teens will bridge their way back into your life. Their peers are unlikely to pose any problem at all.

So stay in touch with your teens during these turbulent times of adolescence. Not since their preverbal years have your children needed more frequent contact with you. Any quality time that they have with you is important. If at all possible at least one parent needs to be at home when your teens come in from school. This allows for invaluable conversation and supervision time. It may be necessary for Mom to stop work for a while to provide this kind of attention.

Spiritual and Moral Development

Your teens are not only interested in guys or gals, and getting out of the family, but they're also interested in God. More people are converted in the years from fifteen to seventeen than at any other similar period in life.

Moral awareness awakens during these years. Curiosity about the supernatural and awe of the eternal break in upon the teenage mind in very impressive ways. Young people take a serious interest in ethics and religion. Moral idealism peaks during this time.

Middle adolescents experience tremendous tension resulting from their spiritual discovery. For the first time in their lives they are aware of the world that "ought to be." Now they can define this world within their own mind. But they're also in touch with the world that is.

Often, seeing the discrepancies between these worlds, young people become very disenchanted with the hypocrisy of the adult generation. They tend to be blind to their own adolescent hypocrisy, but very conscious of the same failings in their parents' lives.

You need to be as transparent and real as possible with your teens. You can't expect your young person to live a life that you haven't been able to model for them. However, if you're walking honestly and transparently before the Lord, don't underestimate the impact of your example on your teens.

The tension created by the distance between the "ought to be" world and the "real" world often poses great problems for the middle adolescent. The teens most troubled by this tension are likely to resolve it in one of four ways:

1. *They may suffer a serious emotional breakdown.*
2. *They may temporarily withdraw into the drug culture.*
3. *They may convert to some radical form of religion. (This is why many radical forms of religion prey upon the middle adolescent.)*
4. *They may also come into a wonderfully healthy and exciting religious conversion.*

Of course, some adolescents are going to avoid the whole spiritual conflict and plunge themselves into a secular pursuit. But let's believe that your teen is going to make it. He or she is going to make it in wholesome relationships with guys or gals, make it out of the family safely, and find a healthy relationship with God.

Three

I'm the Only One God Has Like Me

―――――◆―――――

People, like snowflakes, are unique. There are no two persons alike. At some time in their late teens, young people make this discovery. As older adolescents, they have grown beyond the need to conform to their peers or contend with their parents and are beginning to emerge from the family as individuals.

They are discovering that they can be enough like their peers and their parents to be comfortable with both and yet different enough from either to have an identity of their own. They are determined to celebrate their uniqueness.

One young lady put it like this, "It's kind of neat. I'm the only one God has like me."

When Your Children Graduate, so Do You!

Your traditional role as a parent is almost done when your son or daughter graduates from high school. Then you begin to lean back and look on with less and less involvement as they begin to make more and more of the choices that will define the kind of adults they will be in the future.

Until each gets far enough along for you to see where he or she is heading, you will have your anxious moments. Believe me, my wife and I know. We have raised three children: a son and two daughters. Our son is a musician. One of our daughters is a business major. The other is a lawyer. As you can see, no two of our children are alike. Although they provided us with some breathless moments as they searched for themselves, once we knew each of them had a clear sense of direction toward a constructive personal future, we began to relax and enjoy their uniquenesses.

No two of your children will make the same choices. Each will forge a unique path. Your confidence in your teen's ability to do this will be gained from the way you see your son or daughter relating to his or her family, friends, future, and faith.

Separation From the Family

During the late teens, after graduating from high school, young people begin to put more distance between themselves and their families. Often this involves acquiring the training necessary to get some marketable skills, getting a job, and moving out on their own.

For young people with academic talent, going to college is probably a wise choice. However this tends to prolong adolescence, since they will be living in the artificial environment of some college campus and will continue to be financially dependent upon you.

When you are paying for your young person's education, naturally you will feel you should have some voice in determining his or her life-style. However, when you try to impose any limits on your son or daughter, these efforts revive the old parent-teen struggles of middle adolescence. Your youngster is likely to fear you will be too restrictive in your demands, and you will tend to feel your teen is not taking his or her educational opportunities seriously enough.

Should this tension develop between you, realize that this struggle is perfectly normal and will probably resolve itself during the later years of college training.

In the meantime, if grades are down and you feel that more interest is being taken in having a good time than in acquiring an education, you can always threaten to stop paying for your teen's schooling. This usually produces an acceptable compromise.

THERE IS NO FREE LUNCH! Some teens decide to get a job after graduating from high school. When this is the case, it is usually best if they move into their own apartments. This is especially wise when there are younger children in the home.

After all, the older child will want to live by a different set of rules than those appropriate during high school, and this is to be expected. Often, however, younger brothers and sisters will contend for the same freedom, even though they are not out of school and supporting themselves.

If you should allow your teens to continue living at home after they graduate from high school and become employed, make it clear that they will be charged some reasonable fee for their room and board. Very few people appreciate what is given to them—children are not exceptions to this.

The sooner in life your children learn that there is no free lunch, the more realistically they can face their futures. Of course, if your children want to pay their own way through college and are saving their earnings toward this goal, you may want to contribute the rent you charge toward this project. Nevertheless, charging rent is still wise. This helps young people develop a wholesome sense of responsibility. Then, when you decide to donate the rent to their college funds, the money will be seen more as a generous gift than as something you owe them.

Adopting a practice like this with your first child allows the others to know in advance what will be expected of them. After all, you should be reluctant to do for any of your children what you cannot do for all of them, unless you have a youngster who is handicapped in some way, and then your other children should understand your special treatment of that child.

WHEN COLLEGE IS CLOSE TO HOME. Sometimes children continue to live at home while they go to a nearby college. If they are willing to contribute what they earn at part-time employment and summer jobs toward the costs of their education, you will probably want to give them their room and board. However, even in these cases, you should agree on certain house rules they will be expected to keep and assign them specific household tasks to perform so they can assume some responsibility for their care.

Once young people become financially independent, the struggle with their parents tends to end. In recognizing their responsibility for the governing decisions of their lives, young people realize that problems aren't visited on us by our parents. They are the natural consequences of our own choices.

UNHAPPY MATES OFTEN CLING TO ADULT CHILDREN. When grown children who have full-time jobs continue to live with their parents, one may suspect an unhappy parental marriage. Several years ago, I saw a couple in their early sixties. They were professional people. They had two sons in their late twenties who were still living at home. Neither son was married.

Once I got into the dynamics of the case, I understood why the sons were living at home. One was the favorite of the father, and the other was the favorite of the mother—very much like the family of Isaac and Rebekah (Genesis 25:28).

As soon as the boys were out of high school, their parents bought new automobiles for them and promised them free room and board if they would continue living at home. It didn't take the young men very long to discover they were being treated to a style of life they couldn't afford on their own, and they loved it!

Their father and mother didn't want to be left at home alone with each other. Having one or both of their sons in the house helped them to avoid their differences. As you can see, this was a very destructive relationship for everyone involved.

Remaining dependent upon their parents was certainly not in the best interests of the sons. They lived up everything they made and indulged in all their parents gave them. Under these circumstances, how could they ever be expected to acquire the financial responsibility necessary to have families of their own?

Of course, as long as the children were in the home, Mom and Dad could continue to think of themselves as parents and thus avoid the discomfort of having to learn how to get along with each other as husband and wife. The family system helped the parents deny their marriage problems and kept their sons from discovering the satisfaction of being responsible for themselves.

Finally, an Identity of His Own!

Until your young people leave home they are known primarily as your children. However, once they are away from the family, young people begin to develop a new appreciation for their own identity. They are no longer in competition with brothers and sisters for status in the family. For the first time, they have an established identity of their own in the community.

As they discover what it means to be responsible for themselves, they develop a new appreciation for what their parents have done for them. They begin to relate to you on a more equal basis—like a junior partner in the family firm.

This is really a rewarding time for parents. Once my wife and I had launched our children into futures of their own, it was refreshing to welcome them back home—more as younger peers than as dependent children.

CHILDREN ARE TO OBEY AND HONOR THEIR PARENTS. The Bible gives us a two-stage developmental relationship between children and parents. You'll find it in Ephesians 6:1–3. Here's what Paul says:

> Children, obey your parents in the Lord: for this is right.
> Honour thy father and mother; which is the first commandment with promise; That it may be well with thee, and thou mayest live long on the earth.

As long as children are dependent on their parents and are living at home, they are to obey their parents. Once children move away from home and become responsible for their own lives, they are no longer obligated to obey their parents. However, they are to honor and respect them.

WHEN SHOULD A PERSON BE CONSIDERED AN ADULT? When does a youngster cross that invisible line that changes the obligation from that of obeying his or her parents to honoring them? At what age does this occur? When does a young person become an adult?

One of the frustrations of growing up in America is the lack of a definite way of knowing when one is an adult. It is not easy for a person in our society to know when adult status has been achieved. America has no initiation rites. A young person is not required to pass an examination. Adulthood is not awarded by some conference of the family.

What social measures of adulthood we do have are confusing and obviously designed to benefit the economy and government rather than to help young people celebrate their maturity or welcome them into the adult community. Here are some examples of how confusing state laws are in this regard. You may begin to pay adult prices to get into amusements when you are ten or twelve. In some states, once you are fourteen you may choose which of your parents you want to live with in the event that they divorce. When you are sixteen, you can drive in some states. Once you are eighteen, the law says you are old enough to vote and be drafted. At twenty-one you can establish credit. Now—when are you an adult? At twelve, fourteen, sixteen, eighteen, or twenty-one?

Such legal attempts to define adulthood by the arbitrary choice of some chronological age are bound to be confusing. Obviously you cannot be considered a mature adult until you learn how to take care of yourself—physically, emotionally, spiritually, and financially. You're an adult when you're able to assume total responsibility for yourself. After all, isn't that what maturity is all about?

Facing the Future With Confidence

Healthy families motivate their young people to acquire a marketable skill and a sense of vocational direction early in life. Once these young people are out of high school, they begin to use their marketable skills in pursuing their goals. I'll have more to say about this in chapter seven, "What Will My Work Be?"

Acquiring that first job is a big step for every young person. Do you remember how it felt when you drew your first full week's paycheck? Opening your own personal savings and checking accounts adds to that sense of satisfaction.

College-bound youngsters find their first passing grades to be especially satisfying. After all, these were achieved with no parent looking over their shoulders telling them when they had to study, how long they had to study, or what they had to study. They did it all by themselves! They are launching a future all their own.

Once on their own, young people begin to discover new interests. Many of their "discoveries" will be things you tried to draw their attention to when they were in the home. Then they found these things dull and boring. Now, since no one is forcing the issue, they are excited by them.

DO YOU REMEMBER YOUR FIRST CAR AND APARTMENT? One of the big dreams of every young person is to own his or her own car. Once enough money is saved for a down payment and the first year's insurance, don't be surprised if you are asked to cosign the loan. If the young person has proven to be responsible, most parents are willing to do this.

Eventually young people will get their first apartment. It will probably be already furnished. But as finances permit they will begin to add things that they like, things they select, things they buy and pay for. The place begins to look a little more like them. Then they begin to call that place home.

Often, when a girl goes into an apartment of her own, one of the first things she will buy is a puppy or a kitten. Pets have a way of curing the loneliness of an empty apartment. They give you something for which to care.

Encourage Your Teens to Be Friendly

As your teens grow up, notice their social skills. How easy is it for them to build friendships? How many friends do they have? Do they have at least one or two close friends?

The way your teens relate to their friends is going to make a difference in their futures. A person who has the ability to build healthy friendships is likely to be able to build a healthy marriage. In chapter nine, "Healthy Friendships Are Important," I will be dealing with these issues in more detail.

One of my friends has said that marriage is really friendship with sex. A healthy marriage must be more than a friendship, and it must be more than a sexual relationship. It needs to include both.

In our society we tend to place too much emphasis on the sexual dimension of marriage and not enough on the friendship dimension of marriage. Don't misunderstand me. Sex *is* important—it's a vital part of marriage—but the friendship a couple forms in marriage is more important.

I've seen couples in my professional practice who had a great sex life, but they weren't friends, even though they were married. Often when you get to the roots of a relationship like this, you find mates who never learned the art of forming friendships. As teenagers, they never learned how to build friendships or to respond to someone else's friendship.

HOW IS A YOUNG PERSON'S UNIQUENESS SEEN IN HIS FRIENDS? Every healthy person needs some friends. However, the number of them a young person needs will vary from teen to teen. The more people oriented a young person is, the more friends he or she will need and the more active he or she will be with these friends. A more private person will have fewer friends and will tend not to be so socially active. Privacy will be more important.

I'm not suggesting that if you're friendly you don't enjoy privacy or that if you are a private person you don't enjoy some social life. However it is important for young people to bear in mind the degree of sociability they need, so that when they choose to marry they can choose someone whose social needs are similar.

At our counseling center, we often see married couples who are struggling with conflicting social needs. One mate likes privacy, and the other needs an active social life. These differences were obviously present when they were going together, but their importance was overlooked. So Mrs. Friendly winds up married to Mr. Hermit, and their conflicting needs for people and privacy become a source of frustration from the very beginning of their marriage.

Few couples are able to satisfactorily resolve this nagging source of irritation. The marriage is not totally defeated, but each of them is aware of this continuing social incompatibility.

OUR FRIENDS ARE A REFLECTION OF OURSELVES.Take a look at the kind of people your teens choose for friends, because their choice is actually a reflection of their own self-image. Generally the better they feel about themselves, the more wholesome their friends will be. Unfortunately the reverse is also true.

Some parents find this hard to understand. They are very unhappy with the destructive friendships their teens choose. They believe their son or daughter would be a different person if he or she chose better friends. However, it is just the opposite. If the teen had a better self-image, he or she would not choose friends who bring out the worst in him or her.

Young people who feel good about themselves may have casual friends from many walks of life, but they will usually choose their close friends from among those who are like them—spiritually, socially, and intellectually.

Automobiles and Apartments

Young men go about building friendships differently than young women. For example, the single man finds an automobile an important part of his social life. In fact his car often becomes a symbol of himself.

You can learn many things about a young man by taking a careful look at his car. What kind does he drive? Is it a junker? How does he treat his car? Does he keep it clean and shiny? Is the interior cluttered, or is it orderly and clean? Does he buy things to decorate it?

A fellow's car provides a place of privacy for him and his friends. A typical young man will entertain his friends in his car long before he lets them see the place where he lives.

The apartment becomes, for the single young woman, what the automobile is for the single young man. Understanding parents realize this.

Once in a while we run into the old tradition which dictates that a young woman should live at home as long as she remains single. This was the custom when some of us were growing up, but it is one of the many things that greater employment opportunities for women have changed in our society.

In the earlier decades of this century, finding a respectable way to earn enough money to support an apartment was difficult for a young woman. So a single young woman's moral character was suspect if she lived apart from her parents.

Today a growing percentage of our work force is comprised of women. Progress is being made steadily in securing equal pay for them. Therefore, most young women, upon graduating from high school, are as capable as young men of providing an apartment for themselves.

So if your teen is out of high school, employed, and wants to have her own place to live, give her that right. Don't let this matter become a point of contention between you. Get involved in the process. Help her make the transition.

If you can afford it, you may want to pay the first month's rent for her. If the apartment needs redecorating, offer to help her do it.

When your young people choose to live in their own apartments, let them know they are always welcome at their parents' home. A Saturday afternoon with the family or a good Sunday dinner is often a highlight of the week for young people living in their own places.

Just as a young man's car is a reflection of him, you can see a young woman in her apartment. How neatly is it kept? Is the color coordination appropriate? How feminine does it appear? These are all reflections of the single young woman.

Her apartment becomes the place where she's most likely to take her friends. She'll bring girl friends there. She'll bring her boyfriends there—not for any unwholesome purpose—but this is her place. It's her home.

Defining Their Faith

Sometimes it takes years for young people to find a unique faith of their own. These are anxious years for parents.

I remember how difficult it was for my wife and I to be patient with our son during the years of his spiritual search. He used to say to me, when I would become concerned about his church attendance, "Dad, remember, I grew up in a preacher's home. And if I never went to church another day in my life, I've gone to church enough. I've already gone to church more often than most guys will in their whole lifetime."

I had never thought of that, but it is probably true. However most of us as parents are uneasy until we see some spiritual evidence that indicates that our children are building their own unique and responsible faith in Jesus Christ. It is rewarding when parents discover their children's faith is not simply something that has been superimposed on them by their parents, but is a meaningful expression of themselves.

Once he or she is apart from the supervision of the family, the young person's own relationship with God will surface. Once independence is achieved, young people reveal the role faith will have in their futures. When they begin to regularly attend a place of worship, parents can relax and know that their teens have discovered their own spiritual uniqueness. Then moral decisions made on a daily basis are arrived at with no parental eye peering over their shoulders.

Remember, God has no grandchildren. Your relationship with God identifies you as His child. Each of us has to be born into a vital relationship with Him. Nothing is more exciting for parents than to see this happen in the lives of their children.

If that day is a little long in coming for you, don't let the enemy torment you with the fear that it will never come. Don't let him make you think that the unhappy chapter your son or daughter may we writing in his or her life is the end of the book. It's not! There are happier chapters ahead.

You've sown some good seed. You've watered it with your prayers and tears. Now be patient—and watch the Holy Spirit honor the faithfulness of your example.

Your teenager will develop his or her own unique way of following Jesus. Your teen's faith will not be exactly like yours. My children's faith is not exactly like mine. But they have found a reality in Jesus. They have related themselves to God as His son and daughters. And that's what counts with me.

YOUR EXPERIENCES SHAPE YOUR FAITH. Remember, the definition of your faith has evolved as you served God through the day-to-day emergencies, the crises, and just the casual run-of-the-mill things that have come your way. In the same way, your children's faith is also being defined day by day as they serve God through the crises and emergencies in their own lives.

Children are like snowflakes. They're unique. No two are born with the same genetic endowment. No two grow up to be alike.

Even though your children have grown up in the same home, the way each has chosen to respond to your love and discipline and the way each has chosen to respond to the love and discipline of the Lord has given that individual a uniqueness that defines each as his or her own person. No two are alike.

This exciting discovery of our uniqueness is made in the late teens, and it launches us into a lifelong process of becoming the people God knows we can be in Jesus.

Part II
Helping Your Teens Care for Their Bodies and Minds

Four
It's Dumb to Blow Your Mind

——◆——

I never will forget Matt, a handsome and brilliant teenager with a promising future. His family raised him in the church. But he got caught up in the anger and bitterness of the anti-Vietnam movement that swept our country in the 1960s. He left home. His parents didn't know where he was.

Matt was gone for months. No one heard from him. His parents were frantic. Finally, he called them from San Francisco. He had become a part of the Haight-Ashbury scene—where thousands of anti-Vietnam demonstrators gathered to protest the war. Drugs were a way of life in that area. Matt's parents did their best to convince him to come home, but he was determined to stay.

When he finally came home, you should have seen him. I did— and I cried.

Matt had taken every drug on the street. You name it, and he'd tried it. Finally, after so many trips on LSD and other hallucinogens, there was little of his mind left. He never recovered. He's alive, but he's mentally disabled.

Unfortunately, Matt's story is not unique. Every year in our country, thousands of teens still blow their minds on drugs—even without a Vietnam troubling them.

How Can Parents Help?

In many instances, this kind of tragedy can be avoided by parents and teens talking knowledgeably together about drugs and their effects on the brain. The public school is trying to do a good job in educating young people about the risks of drug abuse, but parents also must be involved in this effort.

Your children need to know that you're knowledgeable about drugs. You should be able to detect the early indications that your teenagers may have a drug problem. I will point some of them out for you later in this chapter.

WE ONLY HAVE ONE BRAIN! The human brain is the most highly organized, complex structure to be discovered anywhere in the universe. It's what makes us different from the animals. The brain houses our intelligence and is the physical agent of both the soul and the spirit. So teens must learn the importance of taking good care of the brain.

In 1 Corinthians 6:19, 20 Paul says:

> What? know ye not that your body is the temple of the Holy Ghost which is in you, which ye have of God, and ye are not your own? For ye are bought with a price: therefore glorify God in your body, and in your spirit, which are God's.

The body is supplied with many, many spare parts. We each have two legs, two arms, two ears, two eyes, ten toes, ten fingers—but only one brain.

Once the brain is damaged, the function dependent on that tissue is often permanently lost to the person. It's regrettable when an adult suffers permanent damage to his or her brain, but the tragedy is compounded when this happens to a teenager.

Drugs are our society's greatest threat to your teenager's brain. So let's ask ourselves the obvious question:

Why Do Teens Take Drugs?

Young People Take Drugs Because They Are Accessible

Man's fascination with drugs is nothing new. However the ready access to drugs in our society makes our problem different from that of previous generations.

DRUG ABUSE HAS A LONG HISTORY. Man has a long and infamous history of drug abuse. Marijuana, for example, was described in a Chinese medical book in 2737 B.C.

Alcohol has been abused for centuries. However, the situation became much worse in the nineteenth century when a new process for distilling liquor was invented in England, flooding that country with cheap gin. Alcohol is more accessible to teenagers today than ever before.

Snuff taking has been very popular in western Europe for centuries. I laughed when I ran across this joke about it, which appeared in an 1834 British magazine. A patient asked his doctor, "Is it true, doctor, that snuff destroys olfactory nerves and clogs and otherwise injures the brain?" "Ha-ha," the doctor said. "It can't be true, since those who have any brains at all never take the stuff."

Chewing tobacco has been America's parallel to snuff. By 1884 the annual per capita consumption of chewing tobacco in the United States had reached four pounds.

Shortly after World War I, we had our first national bout with cocaine. It was a serious problem in our country then. During that period medical schools were also a frequent scene of what they called "ether frolics"—medical students would experiment with getting high on ether.

WATCH THE MEDICINE CABINET! In the last ten years, an explosive increase in psychoactive drug taking has occurred among the youth of the United States. Where do young people usually get these drugs?—at home. In fact, a young person's first experience with drugs is likely to have its roots in the family's medicine cabinet.

Are you aware of your family's stock of medication? How long has it been since you counted your pills? If you have teens in your family, you need to check the pills regularly—at least once each week.

Keeping your medication in some place more remote from your teens than the medicine cabinet will lessen the temptation to them considerably. Remember, it's important that your children observe you taking medication only when you are ill.

It is so convenient to pop a pill when you are experiencing low-level pain or when you are having a little difficulty going to sleep. If you have teens in the home, don't forget that they're watching! Your teens will find it difficult to understand why it's okay for you to pop a pill when you're not really that sick, but it is not okay for them to take a pill when they want to feel better.

If you don't medically need the pills, don't take them. Remember, your teens are watching you and your medicine cabinet all the time. They are discovering whether drugs are used as a convenient way for you to escape the unpleasantness of life or whether they are only used when essential to your health.

The simplest step parents can take toward keeping their teens free from drugs is to keep prescription drugs out of their reach. Regardless of how secretly you may think you have hidden them, take inventory frequently.

Teens Take Drugs Because of Peer Pressure

In some areas, 80 percent of high-school children have used one or more drugs for no medical purpose at all.[5] With this many young people popping pills, you can imagine the group pressure that is on teenagers to experiment with drugs.

Teens bring pills to school they have taken from the family medicine cabinet. Then they exchange pills with their friends. Many times, they don't even know what they're taking. They just take the pills because their friends have told them about the great trip the pills gave them.

Many young people begin their experience with drugs by smoking pot with a boyfriend or girl friend. It's kind of a pact of friendship. Pot parties are often held in the home of a friend whose parents are going to be away for the evening.

This is one reason for knowing the families of your children's friends. You need to know how carefully their parents supervise them. Discourage friendships with young people whose parents give them little supervision.

Young People Take Drugs to Rebel Against Their Parents

Young people can learn to assert their independence in far less destructive ways than in drug abuse. If young people want to rebel against their parents, they need to find a safer way of doing it than by damaging their brains and destroying their futures.

Later, I will devote a whole chapter to helping parents learn some things they can do to get a young person through rebellion when it can't be avoided.

Some Young People Take Drugs to Escape From Reality

Until these teens give evidence of experiencing life more comfortably, they need to be monitored carefully for suicidal risks.

DON'T TAKE CHANCES WITH YOUR TEEN'S LIFE! Remember, suicide is the second highest cause of death among teenagers. Evidences of deep depression or any talk about committing suicide should be taken seriously.

A young person in this much pain needs to be evaluated by a professional person. If you do not know a psychiatrist or psychologist to whom you could take your young person, your pediatrician or family doctor can arrange an appropriate referral for you.

WHY WOULD SOMEONE SO YOUNG BE IN THAT MUCH PAIN? Usually these young people are suffering from some kind of family conflict or broken love relationship.

Frequently, their parents are caught up in a painful marital disturbance. The anxiety and hostility generated between warring mates creates a painful climate from which their teenagers often want to escape. When you and your mate are going through a difficult time in your marriage, be thoughtful enough to help your teens understand it is not their fault. Be sure they know that both their parents love them.

Of course a parental divorce can be very disturbing for young people. After all, their home is being destroyed by two people they love very much, and they feel caught in the middle. Drugs offer temporary relief from such a devastating scene. This is why the wise single parent occasionally has a heart-to-heart talk with his or her teens. They need to understand that it is not their fault their parents' marriage fell apart. Whenever possible, young people need the support of an unbroken love relationship with both parents.

As a single parent, let your children know you are doing your best to provide them a home. Admit you can't be two parents. Hope they will understand. Give them an opportunity to share their pain with you. Remember, parental divorces not only hurt parents, but they also are very painful to teenagers.

Broken teen love affairs can also send young people to the pill bottle. So if you know that your daughter has fallen head over heels in love with someone who has recently rejected her, and she seems to be more moody and withdrawn than usual, give her some special attention and be particularly careful of the family medicine cabinet. Be just as careful with your son when a girl breaks his heart.

Emotionally Disturbed Young People Take Drugs

Chronic feelings of rejection by the family and by friends are usually major factors in a disturbance that happens so early in life.

These are the young people who are most likely to be addicted to drugs.

What Parents Should Know About Drug Abusers

Drug abusers can be divided into three groups:

1. THE CASUAL USER—THE "EXPERIMENTER." These teens use drugs sparingly, primarily to solidify group membership. That is, they want to be in tight with their friends. If their friends use drugs, they will use drugs.

The "experimenter" also may use drugs partially to allay the developmental anxieties accompanying newfound freedom from the family. When he or she was younger, parents provided most of the structure for his or her life. Now the teen must take over more and more of these functions, and that can be nerve-racking.

Casual users often feel there's no middle road with drugs. They must either be "straight," "square," and suspect to many of their friends, or a card-carrying "head."

2. THE SOCIOLOGICAL USER—THE "SEEKER." Some of our brightest youngsters get caught up in this adventurous counterculture. They are searching for a "new" feeling.

Youth's fascination for the new and different makes them particularly vulnerable. When they are told that a trip on this drug will open up new worlds for them, they are ready to go.

This curiosity about different experiences can be seen early in life. For example, it is not unusual for children to spin around in circles until they get so dizzy they can't walk straight; something about the dizzy feeling fascinates them.

The "seeker" continues to be attracted to experiences that promise something different.

3. THE SICK USER—THE "HEAD." Here are some ways to identify the sick user:

There will be serious deficiencies in his interpersonal relationships. He won't get along well with his friends or his parents.

He will have a high frequency of drug use or will rely heavily upon drugs in times of stress.

He prefers the pleasure of drugs to the pleasure of interpersonal relationships. He would rather be "high" on drugs than enjoy recreational activities with his friends.

He is very critical of those aspects of society that are related to his personal problems. If he is having problems with his parents, he is very critical of the family. If he is having problems with his teachers, he is very critical of school.

If these four kinds of problems are not characteristic of your teen, then you can be relatively sure he (or she) is not a "head"—a sick user of drugs.

On the other hand, if you suspect that your teen *is* a sick user of drugs, then you will want to read the last part of this chapter carefully and take the practical steps outlined there to get help for your teen.

Degrees of Drug Involvement

Involvement with drugs can be viewed on a continuum ranging from experimentation to addiction.

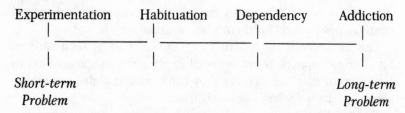

Notice, experimentation is really a short-term problem. It is cause for concern on the part of parents, but not cause for panic.

On the other hand, addiction is a long-term problem. Although panicking is not going to do anyone any good, when you're dealing with an addicted teenager you know you have a serious problem on your hands.

Prolonged experimentation leads to habituation. At some point, taking drugs becomes a habit for young people. Unless that habit is broken it will lead to dependency upon drugs. Young people can stop at any of these stages. But once they move beyond experimentation toward habituation, teens increase their risk of becoming more and more dependent and gradually sliding into addiction.

Let me review these four stages of drug involvement with you:

Experimentation involves the occasional misuse of drugs.

Habituation is indicated when a drug is used regularly.

A state of *dependency* has been reached when the person is psychologically incapable of giving up the drug. At this stage users will promise you they're going to quit. They declare they will never do it again and may be well intentioned in this promise. However, they can't keep this promise, because they have become dependent on the drug.

Addiction is indicated by a pattern of compulsive drug use that includes both physical and psychological dependence. Physiological addiction occurs when the user's body chemistry adapts to the drug and requires it in order for the person to function. When the person is psychologically addicted, he or she cannot function without the drug, even though there is no evidence that the body's chemistry has adapted to it. In either event, the person is totally dependent on the drug. He or she is hooked.

Classifications of Abused Drugs

The three major classifications of abused drugs are depressants, stimulants, and hallucinogens. Now let's take a look at each of these major categories.

Depressants

NARCOTICS. Among depressants, narcotics are the most physically addicting. They induce reverie, while providing relief from pain and anxiety. The more popular narcotics include:

1. Opium, *which is derived from the opium poppy.*
2. Morphine, *a painkiller derived from opium and named after the Greek god of dreams, Morpheus.*
3. Heroin, *also derived from opium and a more powerful painkiller than morphine.*
4. Codeine, *another derivative of opium used for pain relief.*
5. Demerol, *a synthesized pain reliever.*
6. Methadone, *a synthetic chemical that satisfies the addict's craving for narcotics, but does not induce reverie.*

BARBITURATES. The whole family of barbiturates form another group of depressants whose main function is to relieve tension and induce relaxation and sleep. Withdrawal from these drugs without medical supervision can be fatal. These include:

1. *Nembutal.*
2. *Seconal.*
3. *Phenobarbital.*
4. *Butiserpine.*

ALCOHOL. The depressant most abused by young people is alcohol. I will have much more to say about teen abuse of alcohol.

Stimulants

These drugs present the user with energy, alertness, and feelings of confidence. The two most commonly used legal stimulants in our society are:

1. *Nicotine.*
2. *Caffeine.*

AMPHETAMINES. The illegal stimulants sold among our youth are *amphetamines*. These are a group of synthetic drugs that tend to dispel feelings of boredom and weariness.

Some of the common ones are:

1. *Benzedrine.*
2. *Dexedrine.*
3. *Methedrine.*

COCAINE. This is the most popular illegal stimulant on the street. It is produced from the active ingredient in the coca shrub and gives the user a feeling of omnipotence and euphoria unsurpassed by any other drug.

According to surveys, more than one in four people between the ages of eighteen and twenty-five report that they have tried cocaine.[6] A debate continues over whether cocaine is physically addictive, but little doubt exists about the profound psychological addiction users develop.

Hallucinogens

These drugs act on the central nervous system in such a way as to distort sensory perceptions. Some idea of their popularity is indicated by the fact that 5 percent of Americans over the age of twelve have tried one of the major hallucinogens. Major hallucinogens are:

1. Mescaline, *which is derived from the peyote cactus.*
2. Psilocybin.
3. LSD (lysergic acid diethylamide), *a drug synthesized by Albert Hoffman, a Swiss chemist, in 1938. The street name for LSD is "acid." It soon became known as a psychotomimetic drug because it mimics the effects of psychosis.*
4. PCP (phencyclidine) *is an extremely dangerous hallucinogen that often stimulates violent and destructive reactions from its users.*

Minor hallucinogens are much more popular than the major ones. The most common include:

1. Marijuana, *derived from the leaves of the cannabis plant, which grows both wild and cultivated in many countries, including the United States.*

2. Hashish, *which comes from the resin of the cannabis plant and is five to six times stronger than marijuana.*

Approximately one out of every three youngsters above the age of twelve has tried marijuana.[7]

The Biggest Threat to Teenagers Is Alcohol

Alcohol is the drug that poses the biggest threat to your teenager. Twenty-five percent of teenagers drink on a weekly basis and consume two to four drinks once each week. Over 3 million teenagers in the United States have been treated for alcoholism.

The frequency with which teenagers drink and the amount they drink tend to increase steadily through their teen years. Nearly 40 percent of teenagers claim to be nondrinkers at age thirteen. However by the time they reach eighteen only 10 percent claim they have never tried alcohol.

Almost one-half of adolescent suicides involve intoxication. Each year approximately 20,000 teenager drivers are involved in fatal accidents. The majority of these accidents also involve alcohol.

Drinking also plays a major role in the initial sexual experiences of teenagers. Over one-half of our teens are sexually active. Alcohol abuse plays a major role in encouraging sexual promiscuity, unwanted pregnancies, venereal disease, and forced sex or rape. Over 70 percent of those sexually active teens initially experience sex while under the influence of alcohol.[8]

THE BIG RISK IS IN JUNIOR HIGH SCHOOL! The average age at which a youngster first abuses a drug, whether alcohol or some other drug, is 11.9 years for boys and 12.7 years for girls.

Our concerns need to be focused on junior-high youth. Drug abuse is most likely to start at this time. It is regrettable that we have to worry about such a serious problem plaguing children so early in life, but this is where the focus of much of the drug traffic is today.

A Checklist for Parents

Here are some questions to help you to determine whether drug or alcohol abuse is a problem for your teenager:

1. *Has there been any marked change in your teenager's regular habits and activities?*
2. *Has your teenager had any trouble at school or with the police, which cannot be easily explained?*
3. *Have there been absences from school without satisfactory explanations?*
4. *Is your teenager doing his or her schoolwork?*
5. *Has your teenager abandoned old friends in favor of others who are inclined to drink and hang around questionable people and places?*
6. *Has your teenager reported any memory blanks? These could indicate "blackouts," one of the early signs of alcoholism.*
7. *Is your teenager spending large amounts of money for which he or she cannot account?*
8. *Is your teenager reluctant to discuss alcohol and other drug problems with you?*
9. *Are you aware of rumors about how much your teenager is partying?*
10. *Do you have any evidence that your teenager may be drinking alone or sneaking drinks before going out?*

Take a careful look at these questions and breathe a sigh of relief if you can conscientiously say, "I know my teenager well, and none of these apply." On the other hand, you may find yourself saying, "Yes, several of these are real, vital issues in my teen's life."

In that event, let me urge you to carefully investigate the situation. If you discover your teenager is involved with drugs, get help from a competent Christian mental-health professional in devising a strategy for dealing effectively with the problem.

How Can the Drug Abuser Be Helped?

To know that your young person is on drugs is one thing; discovering what you can do about it is another.

Until drug users want help, no one can help them—not even God! This inability to help is not because they cannot be helped, but because they *will not* be helped.

Often people with drug-abuse problems have to get worse before they can get better. This is particularly true of alcoholics. Trying to help them before they have reached the end of themselves is futile. Premature efforts will prove to be very frustrating and disappointing.

Teen Challenge, one of this country's most successful drug rehabilitation programs has discovered the important role a personal faith in Christ plays in the recovery of drug abusers. In the Teen Challenge approach, the person experiences a new beginning in Jesus.

The idea of a new beginning becomes one of the most effective means of breaking the chain drugs have forged around a teenager's mind. Then a divine strength is relied upon to reinforce the person's damaged will and pull the user out of slavery to the drug.

Rehabilitation is more likely to be successful with young people whose families are supportive. If your young person has a drug problem, by all means let your teen know the security of your love and do your best to help your son or daughter.

You can't help your teen until he or she is ready to be helped, but if your child is ready to be helped, by all means make yourself available in any way possible. Get involved in a treatment program with your teen. Don't hesitate to get the professional help your youngster may need. These problems are not self-correcting. Time alone won't make them better.

Here are some things teenagers will need in a successful rehabilitation program:

> Self-acceptance needs to be available to them.
> Their self-esteem needs to be respected.
> They need encouragement in building interpersonal relationships.
> The program should involve sexual education and counseling.

They will need help in returning to school when they come out of the program.

They will need vocational guidance.

These are the features you should look for in trying to select a treatment program for your youngster.

If you discover your teenager is involved with drugs, don't panic. Surface the subject for discussion and be sure of your facts. In most cases, you will be relieved to find your youngster is only involved in experimentation. Though this is a cause for concern, it isn't reason for panic.

Remember, many of us experimented with some form of drugs in our adolescence, and we turned out okay. Just get your teenager the help he or she needs. Commit your child to the Lord. Believe God to see you and your teenager through this problem.

Five

Looking Forward to Marriage

———◆———

When God created people, He made them male and female. This is part of what He called "very good" when He, with pleasure, smiled over His creation. In Genesis 1:31 Moses describes it this way: "And God saw every thing that he had made, and, behold, it was very good. And the evening and the morning were the sixth day."

God created sex! So how can there be anything essentially evil or dirty about it?

Yet most Christians I counsel have had to come to terms with guilt feelings about their sexuality. Often these feelings can be traced back to ways they learned to feel and think about their sexuality earlier in life.

God wants your teenager to be comfortable with his or her sexuality. You can help your child achieve this goal.

Sexual Identity

Young people need to know that God made us body persons. He formed our bodies from the dust of the earth and breathed a part of Himself into them.

YOUR BODY IS AS DIVINE AS YOUR SPIRIT. Many times we are left with the impression that our spirit is more divine than our bodies. This is certainly not a biblical idea. Your teens need to understand that our bodies are as much God's gift to us as are our spirits. This is what the doctrine of the resurrection is all about.

If the body were evil, the grave would be its end. There would be no resurrection of the righteous dead. However the hope of the New Testament believer is anchored in the resurrection of the dead (1 Corinthians 15).

The body identifies us as human beings. When God wanted to become human, even He had to assume a body. This is what the incarnation is all about: "And the Word was made flesh, and dwelt among us . . ." (John 1:14).

Healthy young people do not feel guilty about their bodies, nor are they afraid of them. Your role as a parent is very important in teaching your teens how to be comfortable with their bodies.

OUR SEXUALITY IS PART OF GOD'S IMAGE IN US! God deliberately chose to make us like Himself. This involved making us sexual. In Genesis 1:27 Moses says, "So God created man in his own image, in the image of God created he him; male and female created he them."

Carl Barth, famous theologian, went so far as to say that our sexuality *is* the Godlikeness in us. Before you are too critical of him, reflect, for a moment, on how the heavenly and the human meet in man's sexuality. Perhaps a man and a woman are never more like God than when, in love, they create life. That act of creation is a function of our sexuality.

GOD MADE US BODY PERSONS. You cannot know yourself without coming to terms with your body—getting to know yourself as a sexual person. This need not have anything to do with intercourse. A person is a sexual being, even if he or she never chooses to have sexual intercourse.

INTERCOURSE IS FOR MARRIAGE! On the other hand, in our day, many attempt to find their identity and satisfaction in life by hopping from one bed to another. Few things could be more devastating to a person or more disappointing in the search for fulfillment in life.

Your teen needs to know that sexual intercourse is a life-uniting act that becomes destructive in any other context but marriage.

YOUR SEXUALITY IS RELATED TO YOUR IDENTITY. Your teen's sexuality is deeply related to his or her personhood. Although being a person taps a deeper part of me than just being a male, I cannot define my personhood without involving my maleness. Those who know me, know me as a male.

So learning how to be comfortable with your body is an important part of knowing yourself. How comfortable are you with your body? If you have made a friend of your body, your children will feel at home more easily with their bodies.

YOUR BODY MAKES A DIFFERENCE IN YOUR POINT OF VIEW. Your teens should know that a person who lives in a body of the opposite sex will see things differently from the way those of their sex do. Becoming aware of this early in life will help them develop a much needed appreciation for the differences between a male's point of view in life and a female's point of view.

These differences are where many married couples have a parting of the ways. The man doesn't understand how the world looks to a woman, and the woman doesn't understand how it looks to a man.

Growing up male gives men a different perspective on life from that of women, who have been socialized as females. Neither is necessarily right. Each is simply different from the other. Knowing this helps tremendously in facilitating understanding between a man and a woman.

Feeling good about being male or female and developing an appreciation for the other's point of view are essential parts of a healthy sexual identity.

As a parent, you play a key role in helping your teen find a comfortable sexual identity. Encourage your son to learn from young women what life is like from a woman's point of view. Encourage your daughter to learn from young men what life is like from a man's point of view. If each parent did this, young men and women would enter marriage understanding that they see the same world from two very different points of view. Neither would see the other's point of view as wrong—simply different. What a tremendous advantage this would give them in building a strong and healthy marriage!

Sexual Behavior

Young people need to know that Jesus lived in a real, live male body. His body had flesh and bones, just as we have. His glands and hormones were as active as yours and mine.

This is why He can be " ... touched with the feeling of our infirmities ... " and " ... was in all points tempted like we are, yet without sin" (Hebrews 4:15). You might show your teens this passage so they will understand that Jesus is in touch with their humanity—He understands their sexuality. He can help them manage it.

Jesus did not experience genital sex, but this does not mean that He had no erotic feelings. He must have had erotic feelings, because He was tempted in all points like we are. If He had no erotic feelings, this would have been impossible.

Jesus related to men and women as a male. The author of *Jesus Christ Superstar* imagines this to have posed real problems for Mary Magdalene.

You remember her profession; she was a prostitute. The familiar ways she knew how to love a man involved genital sex. She knew this kind of love was not an appropriate way to express appreciation to her Lord for casting the demons of lust out of her life. So she expresses her frustration in being unable to properly love this man who saved her from a life of prostitution by singing, "I Don't Know How to Love Him."

People who can only love in a sexual way are too emotionally handicapped to succeed in marriage. Therefore your teen needs to learn how to express love in ways that do not involve genital sex.

PORNOGRAPHY IS EVERYWHERE! You need to be aware of the sexual scene your children are confronted with everyday. Pornography is readily available to young people in public schools. In fact, by the time they are out of junior-high school, over half of both males and females have been exposed to pornographic books and magazines. This may come as a shock to you, but if you are close enough to your teens for them to be open and honest with you about sexual matters, you know this to be true.

By the time they become adults, 85 percent of young men and 70 percent of young women have been exposed to some form of X-rated material.[9]

Why do teens get involved in pornography and X-rated movies? Teenagers have always been very curious about sex. Sexual exploration and experimentation are prominent throughout the adolescent years. This is why parental supervision of teenage activities is so important. If you want to minimize this curiosity and experimentation, you will see that your teenagers are adequately supervised.

HOW SHOULD PARENTS REACT TO SEXUALLY COMPROMISING SITUATIONS? Finding young people in some kind of sexual activity creates a very awkward and disturbing scene for everyone involved. How should you react to it?

Let me say this is always cause for concern. But panic never helps anyone—the young people or the parents.

Should this happen to you, withdraw from the scene as discreetly as possible. Later, after everyone has had a chance to regain composure, engage in a healthy dialogue with your teen about the sexual risks such experimentation involves and the wisdom of heeding the biblical admonition to reserve deeper sexual intimacies for marriage.

EXPLAIN THE PRACTICAL REASONS FOR PREMARITAL CHASTITY. Notice I said *dialogue*. Engage your young person in meaningful, factual, conversation about adolescent sexual morality, but don't preach. Preaching is not going to help, it will only drive your adolescent farther from you.

What you want is the kind of open, confidential relationship that leaves your teens feeling free to come to you when they have questions or are in some kind of moral conflict. Keep an openness between you and your teens about sexual morality.

Remember, most of us engaged in some kind of sexual experimentation when we were in our teens. Don't share the details of these struggles with your teens, but do let them know that you had to deal with many of these same issues—and the Lord saw you through! Assure them that He will also see them through these temptations.

THINGS ARE DIFFERENT TODAY! The sexual scene of today's teens is very different from the one we knew when we were growing up.

Here are some startling statistics to describe some of these differences.

In 1981 parents were shocked to read that, of the 29 million thirteen- to nineteen-year-olds in the United States, 12 million had experienced their first sexual intercourse. The average age of first intercourse was sixteen; by age nineteen four-fifths of boys and two-thirds of girls have had intercourse. Based on these statistics, four out of every ten fourteen-year-old girls will become pregnant at least once during their teen years. Two out of every ten will have a baby and about one in seven will have an abortion.[10]

If your young people are to successfully avoid being caught up in this popular mood, they will need some healthy guidelines to follow in their dating practices. I will be suggesting some in chapter ten, which deals with mate selection.

Sexual Morality

The sexual morality of your teens will be a product of their home and church. This means that you should be prepared to have some open, frank, and honest discussions with them about the sexual realities of life. Let me give you some biblical guidelines for your conversations. First of all, read 1 Corinthians 6:13–7:5 as frequently as is necessary for you to be thoroughly familiar with the passage. This is the longest statement in the New Testament about God's purpose for making us body persons. Here Paul articulates the New Testament theology of the body.

The passage contains three simple but very important biblical statements to guide Christians in managing their sexual behavior.

The Body Is Not for Fornication

In other words, your body is not designed to find lasting fulfillment in sexual experiences with a variety of partners outside of marriage. If it were, the happiest people in the world would be the most sexually promiscuous among us. No thinking person believes this to be true. However, this is the lie foisted upon the public by pornographers. Ever since Adam, there have been those foolish enough to believe it until their lives have been painfully damaged trying to prove it.

THE SECULAR WORLD IS MORE AND MORE ACCEPTING OF FORNICA-TION. Today's generation has invented a vocabulary that permits the secular person to talk about fornication in morally permissive and socially euphemistic terms. For example, few secular people talk about prostitutes. Instead, they refer to "commercial" or "recreational" sex.

In any major city of this country, places are available where a person's desires for sexual variety and preference become options he selects in buying an evening of "sexual fun," much the same way he would select the ingredients in ordering a pizza. Unfortunately, for many Americans, sex has become this kind of sick recreation and entertainment.

Furthermore, many people become indignant if you even insinuate that healthy sex and love are inseparable. They resent having to profess love for a person before having sex with him or her. These advocates of "casual sex" see intercourse as a legitimate way for a couple to end an evening together. For them intercourse is a form of communication between two people, only slightly more intimate than holding hands or kissing.

The terms *commercial sex, recreational sex,* and *casual sex* are deceitful and devastating misnomers. Attempts at treating sex casually or recreationally before marriage can permanently damage a person's sexual health. Sexual promiscuity often becomes a habit that marriage does not break. Discovering this after marriage is tragic!

WHAT IS DIFFERENT ABOUT THE SINS OF FORNICATION? In the face of some temptations, believers are admonished, "Submit yourselves therefore to God. Resist the devil, and he will flee from you" (James 4:7). However, when confronted with fornication, the believer is encouraged to flee. Why are sins of fornication to be treated differently?

Paul understood the risks involved in sexual misbehavior. That is why he issues this warning to his Corinthian readers, "Flee fornication. Every sin that a man doeth is without the body; but he that committeth fornication sinneth against his own body" (1 Corinthians 6:18).

SINS OF FORNICATION ARE AGAINST THE BODY. Because a person's sexual preferences later in life often come from sexual attitudes and appetites created earlier in life, his or her early attitudes and appetites need to be healthy. After all, these determine your body's sexual needs and sexual expressions.

A person has sinned against his or her body when he or she develops sexual attitudes and appetites before marriage that are inconsistent with an expression of healthy sexuality in marriage. Such a person has not properly prepared his or her body for bonding with a mate.

More than a few marriages are victims of such sins. For example, when a woman enters marriage with negative attitudes toward sex, she is often responding to residual anger toward men who pressured her for sexual favors earlier in her life. She may also be responding to unresolved guilt for having given in to them. Unless she comes to terms with these indignations and offenses in a constructive way before she marries, she is likely to have difficulty forming a healthy sexual bond with her mate.

Here is another example. When a man cannot be sexually true to his mate, the problem often occurs because his promiscuous premarital ways have created appetites for a variety of sexual expressions that marriage doesn't satisfy. Promiscuity has become a habit that marriage can't break. By continually overriding his conscience in sexually tempting situations, he has successfully seared it.

SEXUALITY AND BONDING ARE INSEPARABLE. God built into our bodies the ability to bond to another. Our sexuality is inextricably related to this ability. We cannot express ourselves sexually without affecting the bonding ability of our bodies. This is why Paul says, "What? know ye not that he which is joined to an harlot is one body? for two, saith he, shall be one flesh" (1 Corinthians 6:16). A man who treats sex casually or recreationally jeopardizes his bonding ability. The laws God has created within his body continue to function, even if his partner is a prostitute. Each successive partner only further compromises his ability to form a permanent bond with his future mate.

Promiscuous behavior creates memories that adversely affect people in many ways. If their experiences are pleasurable, they will have a tendency to long for them and adversely compare their future sexual experiences to them. If their experiences were unpleasant, they will tend to carry that negative bias into future relationships.

Think of the dissatisfaction this can create in marriage! There is no way fornication can be healthy. It is always destructive.

If people treat sex casually or recreationally before they are married, how can they treat it sacredly after they are married? Sexual attitudes and practices are habitual! The sooner in life we understand this, the better care we are likely to provide for our sexuality.

ADHESIVE TAPE IS NOT MADE FOR REPETITIVE USE! Sometimes when I'm talking to teens I draw an analogy between the bonding capability of the body and adhesive tape. The strongest bond adhesive tape is capable of making is formed with the first surface to which it is applied. You can remove the tape and reapply it to other surfaces several times, and it will still adhere. However, with every application some of the adhesiveness has been compromised. Finally, if you continue the practice long enough, there will not be enough adhesiveness left to make the tape stick to any surface.

God intended that the bond between mates be the closest and strongest one they are capable of forming. That is why Paul makes it very clear that the body is not for fornication.

The Body Is for the Lord

The body is made for relationships. That is, in making us body persons, God provided us the possibility of forming an intimate unity with other body persons—a unity similar to that which exists among the Trinity (John 17:21–23). This is a unique reflection of God's image in us.

Your body is designed to provide you the ability to form an intimate bond with your Creator. In fact, the highest purpose of your body is not achieved until God takes up His residence in you and your body becomes the temple of the Holy Spirit.

THE KINGDOM'S PLEASURES ARE GREATER THAN SIN'S PLEASURES. When people perceive the benefits of obeying the gospel to be more desirable than the pleasures of sin, they are ready to open their lives to the Holy Spirit.

What is obeying the gospel? It means that you confess yourself to be a sinner and believe God's good news for sinners, which is that:

1. *Jesus Christ, God's only begotten Son, died to take away the sins of the world (John 3:16, 17).*
2. *Christ's resurrection from the dead proves His death to*

*be accepted by God as a more than sufficient sacrifice for
your sins (1 Corinthians 15:1–17).*
3. *As you are honest with God about your sins, He will be
faithful to forgive you and cleanse you through the blood
of His son, Jesus Christ* (1 John 1:7–9).

Receiving Jesus Christ as your Savior from sin results in your
being born into God's family by an act of His will (John 1:12, 13).
God's Spirit bears witness with your spirit that this new birth has
taken place (John 3:5–8; Romans 8:14–17).

Your awareness of the change reaches deeper than your intellect.
Your spirit is penetrated by God's Spirit. You know your body has
become the temple of the Holy Spirit. Your Creator has moved in
where He belongs (1 Corinthians 6:19, 20). The evidence that His
Spirit dwells in you is to be found in your celebration of Christ's
kingdom, which is one of righteousness, peace, and joy (Romans
14:17).

Christ not only forgives you for your sin, He takes it away. He
makes it possible for you to appear before God in His righteousness.
What a revelation! This is enough to bring peace to any anxious and
guilty heart.

No peace in the world compares with this. We have Jesus' word
on that (John 14:27). Experiencing this peace brings " . . . joy un-
speakable and full of glory" (1 Peter 1:8).

NOTHING CAN COMPARE WITH KINGDOM PLEASURES! Kingdom
pleasures are the most fulfilling and satisfying experiences a person's mind and body can know. They have been designed by God to
bind us to Himself. Once you know these experiences, you are
spoiled for the world. No pleasure of sin can compete with them.

From this bond comes our primary source of happiness; it provides our greatest security. Our identity as children of God is anchored in this bond.

David, a man of the world who had experienced all kinds of pleasures, reminds his readers in Psalms 16:11, ". . . in thy presence is
fulness of joy; at thy right hand there are pleasures for evermore."

When he compared the joys of military conquest, of great music and poetry, of illegitimate sexual pleasures with the joy he experienced in God's presence, there was no contest. Any worldly pleasures are short-lived. Kingdom pleasures are "for evermore."

As pleasurable and exciting as sex in marriage is, it cannot be compared with the peace and joy of the Lord. In experiencing God's presence, your mind and body reach depths of peace and heights of joy no other relationship can provide. The body is not for fornication: the body is for the Lord!

Your Body Is for Your Mate

When you marry, your body is for your mate. Paul says, "The wife hath not power of her own body, but the husband: and likewise also the husband hath not power of his own body, but the wife" (1 Corinthians 7:4).

The first bond we form, when we come into this world, is with our parents—with Mother first, and then with Father. From the ability we acquired in developing close feelings with our parents, we learn to be close to our brothers and sisters.

As we grow out of our family, our ability to form family ties becomes the basis from which we build friendships in the community.

THE MARRIAGE BOND IS MORE IMPORTANT THAN FAMILY TIES. The most important bond we will ever form with another person is the one that will ultimately attach us to our mate in Christian marriage. This bond, secured in sexual union, is to be the strongest of all. When compared to other bonds among family and friends, this is the one most like that between Christ and the church.

The pleasure of sexual orgasm is a divinely provided means of intensifying this bond. Sexual pleasure in marriage is God's reward to a couple who are committed to each other for life. This joy was designed to reinforce the exclusivity of the marital relationship. Anytime sexual intercourse is taken outside of marriage, it violates the purpose it was designed to serve.

As the peace and joy of the kingdom are to bind the believer to Christ so the joy and peace of sexual intercourse are to bind husband and wife together (Ephesians 5:31, 32). The more the divine purpose for this pleasure is compromised in fornication, the less likely it is to reinforce the marriage bond.

INTERCOURSE IS FOR MARRIAGE! So until marriage, lessen the risk of being deeply hurt or deeply hurting someone else by avoiding intercourse. Sublimate sexual energy into a vigorous physical life and care for your own sexual needs.

Since there is a delay of about ten years from the time sexual desires peak in adolescence until the average young man and young woman marry, an extended period of self-discipline is required. As parents, try to understand how difficult it must be to remain chaste in a society as sexually stimulated as ours is. Even though your son or daughter is a Christian, exercising sexual discipline until marriage will be a difficult challenge.

Masturbation and Fantasies

WHAT ABOUT MASTURBATION? In what appears as an act of mercy, God does not mention masturbation in the Bible, nor is there a specific reference to the practice in Scripture. I infer from this that God did not consider this matter critical to our salvation. If He had, I'm sure it would be more directly addressed in Scripture.

Until marriage makes intercourse permissible, masturbation is the simplest and least complicating means of providing sexual release for those whose needs demand it. You should know that 95 percent of teen males and approximately 60 percent of teen females practice masturbation.[11] So you can assume that this practice is highly likely to be a part of your teen's life.

Let your teens know that you understand their sexual struggles. Remind them that you have not always been an adult. Moving from childhood to adulthood also posed moral risks for you. Explore the subject of masturbation with them. Help them to share their feelings about this practice with you. Make it clear to them that this subject is not discussed in the Scriptures. Do not condone masturbation, but don't condemn it either.

Help them understand masturbation as an issue of private conscience like other matters of this nature that Paul deals with in

Romans 14:13–23. None of them are critical to a believer's salvation, but how they are viewed is important to the believer's peace of mind.

HELP YOUR TEEN DEAL WITH MASTURBATORY GUILT. Many young people feel guilty for masturbating. If your son or daughter battles masturbatory guilt, respect his or her conscience. Don't try to persuade your teen not to feel guilty. Simply explain that he or she may seek forgiveness from the Lord Jesus for this guilt as frequently as is necessary.

The practice of masturbation is not physically harmful, but if a young person feels guilty about it and does not know how to receive forgiveness, the unresolved guilt can be responsible for serious emotional problems. For example, those who feel most guilty are going to masturbate more frequently and thus compound the guilt and the damage to their self-image.

Controlling the guilt limits the practice. So teach your young person to confess his or her masturbatory guilt to the Lord. Assure your teen that as often as he or she sincerely confesses, the Lord will be faithful and just in forgiving him or her (1 John 1:9).

ALL SEXUAL FANTASIES ARE NOT SINFUL. Determine if the guilt is related to fantasies your teen may be entertaining during masturbation. In Matthew 5:27, 28, Jesus did warn of the moral danger involved in fantasizing about intercourse with someone to whom we are not married. Fantasies that are pornographic or adulterous are unhealthy and destructive. That is why Jesus called them sin.

However, imagining what intercourse in marriage will be like is not sinful. In fact this kind of nonspecific anticipation of sexual pleasure in marriage can serve as a healthy restraint in helping teens to resist sexual temptations and to determinedly save intercourse for marriage. Encourage your teen to limit his or her fantasies to this kind of healthy anticipation. Assure them that such fantasies are normal and consistent with being Christian.

When you have helped your teenager establish a healthy sexual identity, adopt a wholesome biblical sexual morality, and develop ways of constructively managing sexual behavior, you have taken a great big step toward helping him or her feel comfortable with sexuality.

The other big issue teens often have difficulty with is authority. In the next chapter, I will be giving you some practical suggestions for helping your teens come to terms with it.

Part III

Helping Your Teens Take Control of Their Lives

Six

Coming to Terms With Authority

One of the most important practical lessons we learn during our teens is how to relate successfully to people in authority. Until we get our spurt of adolescent growth, we are so much smaller than those in authority that we really don't have much choice—we have to obey.

Once we are physically as large or larger than those in authority over us, we usually want to test the limits they have set for us. This sets the stage for parent-teen conflict.

Learning to Get Along With the Boss

Often teens mistakenly assume that once they are as big as adults they no longer have to do what they are told. For years they have looked forward to being their own boss, and they may try to celebrate their liberation far ahead of schedule.

Many teens are shocked to discover that a person never gets to the place in life where he or she has no rules to keep, no limits to observe, no boundaries for his or her behavior. Some teens find it difficult to come to terms with the fact that we are always under someone's authority. We will always have rules to keep, laws to obey, bosses and stockholders to please, or boards to whom we must give an account.

Therefore, if your teens are going to experience personal happiness and be even moderately successful in achieving their goals in life, they need to learn how to get along with people in authority and come to terms with the inevitability of limits. What better place is there for helping them learn these valuable lessons in life than home? What more appropriate teachers could they have than their parents?

Transferring Control

Actually, the parent-teen task during adolescence can be seen as a cooperative transfer of control. For several years, in families where parents have been good disciplinarians, this has been gradually taking place.

Success in this operation not only requires adolescents to learn how to relate to those in authority in a congenial and cooperative way, but also confronts them with the task of taking authority over their own lives. They must now begin to assume total responsibility for themselves.

How can parents help their teens manage this transition as smoothly as possible? In the remaining years of your authority over your teens, try following this simple three-F formula:

Be Fair!

Let's take a look at what "being fair" is all about. To begin with, *you*—not your teens—must determine what is fair. After all, it is your responsibility. You are the adult. If teens knew how to be fair and responsible on their own, they wouldn't need parents.

BEING FAIR IS NOT ALWAYS EASY! You cannot determine fairness on the basis of a popular vote by your teens. The nature of adolescents is selfish. This is why, for a time, your definition of *fairness* will often be viewed by your teens as being very unfair.

Therefore, be prepared to be told that you are the strictest parent in the neighborhood, the school district, the church—if not the whole country. If you are going to parent teens successfully, you must be able to endure times when your teens believe they have the world's meanest parents.

Parents who must continually be reassured by their teens that they are great parents are too insecure to make the tough decisions parenting adolescents requires at times. Raising teenagers who become responsible adults is a more important goal than having their continual approval.

Most of us can look back to our teen years and recall how "out of it" we thought our parents were. Now it's our children's turn to think that way about us. They'll get over it—just as we did. Then it will be *their* children's turn!

EACH OF YOUR TEENS IS DIFFERENT. A more practical way of determining what is fair for your teens is to have compassion on them. That is, develop the ability to put yourself in their shoes. Once you are able to do this, you will see your need for a different definition of fairness for dealing with each of your children.

Here are some things to consider when you are determining what is fair. First of all, remember the child's age. A common complaint of young teens is that they can't have the same liberty that their older brother or sister has. However, you and I know that a thirteen-year-old youngster is not ready to responsibly manage the freedom that a fifteen-year-old brother or sister can. So the age of the child is a factor in determining what's fair.

The child's past behavior record must also be considered. Children who have been easily managed can be given more liberty. On the other hand, children who have been difficult need to be given their freedom more slowly and deliberately.

The disposition of the child should also be borne in mind. This is what Solomon was talking about when he said, "Train up a child in the way he should go . . ." (Proverbs 22:6).

Each of your children has a different nature—a different disposition. Each responds differently to your parental efforts to bring a sense of discipline and direction into his or her life. Being sensitive to these differences is an important part of parental fairness.

HOUSE RULES ARE NECESSARY. Because each of us is different, living together in a family requires some house rules—rules everybody agrees to keep. Here is a list I ran across. You may want to post it in two or three prominent places in your home.

1. *If you open it, close it.*
2. *If you turn it on, turn if off.*
3. *If you unlock it, lock it up again.*
4. *If you break it, admit it.*
5. *If you can't fix it, call in someone who can.*
6. *If you borrow it, return it.*
7. *If you value it, take care of it.*
8. *If you make a mess, clean it up.*
9. *If you move it, put it back.*
10. *If it belongs to someone else, be sure to ask for permission before you use it.*
11. *If you don't know how to operate it, leave it alone.*
12. *If it's none of your business, don't ask questions.*

MAKE THE LIMITS FAIR. Establishing limits and responsibilities for teens can be made easier if you do it in a structured and uniform way. Here are some suggestions:

Limits on telephone and bathroom time. Why not adopt some family guidelines for using the telephone? For example, set a limit of ten minutes per call for thirteen- and fourteen-year-old youngsters. Allow middle teens twenty minutes per call and older teens thirty minutes per call. In fact, this is a good limit for Mom and Dad to put on their own calls. Very little benefit comes from telephone conversations that are longer than thirty minutes.

By limiting all family phone conversations in this way, you minimize two other frustrating problems: When family members are away from home, it won't be as difficult to call in; and when they are home, they won't have to wait forever to call out.

You may also need to set a bathroom time limit at twenty minutes. This doesn't rush anybody. It gives everybody the time they need to take care of all the things that are necessary to look good, smell good, and get ready to take on the world.

Curfews and limits on dating schedules. Dating schedules are also going to need limits. Frequently I am called upon to help some parents cool off a love affair in their teen's life that was allowed to begin too early and has gone too far. If you want to avoid this risk to your teen's future, let me offer you the following suggestions.

As a general rule in setting dating limits, be conservative! Remember, giving freedom is easier than recalling it. Once you have allowed your teen freedom to pursue a relationship, you will find it extremely difficult, if not impossible, to break that relationship—regardless of how unhealthy or undesirable it may be. Therefore, initially be conservative! If your teen uses the freedom you give responsibly, you can always be more generous.

Ninth and tenth graders should be able to manage group dates or double dates. Single dating should be reserved for eleventh and twelfth graders.

Here are some suggested curfew limits for your young people. Ninth- and tenth-grade girls should be home by 10:30 at night during the week and 11:00 P.M. on weekends. Guys will need about a half hour more, since they need time to get home after they take the young lady home.

Once your daughters are in the eleventh grade, a reasonable limit is 11:30 P.M. during the week and midnight on weekends. Remember, your sons will need a half hour longer to get home.

Twelfth-grade girls should be home by midnight during the week and 12:30 A.M. on weekends. Your sons should be expected a half hour later.

You may have a hard time making these curfews stick, but even your eleventh and twelfth graders know that after one o'clock in the morning, nothing constructive is happening in the community.

What about allowances? Allowances are an excellent way to teach teens responsibility. You can learn much about your teens by observing their stewardship of money. Are they conscientious tithers? How carefully do they plan their budgets? Are they impulsive spenders? Do they share what they have with others? How self-indulgent are they?

Your family income should be borne in mind when setting the limit of your teens' allowances. Older children should be allowed more, because usually their expenses are greater.

Don't give your teenagers allowances they haven't earned. One of the most important lessons for living that you can teach them is if you don't earn your allowance, you don't get it. Unearned allowances are forfeited. The sooner in life your teen learns there is no "free lunch," the more wisely he or she will be prepared to face the future.

Don't be timid in setting these limits for your teens. Teens need limits. They won't always like them. They may want to test them, but they need them. It is important for them to know that just as you have tried to be fair in setting these limits, you intend to see that they are firmly enforced. Coming to terms with this type of parental authority helps prepare your teens for coming to terms with the limits in the everyday world of their adult lives.

HELP YOUR TEENS BECOME RESPONSIBLE ADULTS. Your teens are going to need to learn the difference between rights and privileges. So first of all, let me define what I mean when I talk about *rights*. Your teen's rights are those things essential to life: health care, food, shelter, education, church attendance (not social events in church, but worship services and training programs).

On the other hand, privileges include an allowance, access to the family car, extra wardrobe, extended curfews, and outings with their friends. These are not rights; they are privileges. If privileges are earned, they are granted. If they are not earned, they should not be granted. Isn't that simple?

How are privileges earned? Privileges are earned by being responsible. From early childhood children should be given increasing responsibility for themselves and their space in the home. Once youngsters are teens, they should keep their own rooms clean. Teens should also be helping to care for the shared areas of the home—bathrooms, kitchen, family room, basement, garage, patio, yard, and so on.

The responsibilities assigned each child should be agreed upon by the parents. Don't expect your children to be happy about these. Typically, they are going to think that you always let their brother or sister get off with less work. Remember how it was when you were a teen? If there were other children in the family, didn't you complain because you thought more was required of you than of them? Young people have always thought that the parent gives their brother or sister the easier task and puts the heavier load on them. So don't expect your children to be happy about the responsibilities you give them, anymore than they are happy about the limits you set for them.

After all, you are preparing them to grow up into a real world where the limits that will be set for them and the responsibilities that will be required of them will not always be designed with their "happiness" in mind. So by ignoring their criticisms and complaints, holding to the fair limits you have set for them, and requiring them to assume the responsibilities you have assigned them, you are helping them to stretch and grow into adults who will know how to deal with the limits and responsibilities in the real world.

Be Firm!

Remember, your teens don't have to think the limits you set for them are fair, only you do. They don't have to think the responsibilities you give them are fair, only you do. If young people knew how to set healthy limits for themselves and were mature enough to assume their fair share of family responsibilities without someone else requiring them to do that, why would they need parents?

If you know you are setting fair limits and you know that the responsibilities you are setting are fair, then don't argue those issues with your teens. Simply state where the limits are, explain what the responsibilities are, and require your teens to come to terms with these limits and responsibilities.

Once you know you are a fair parent, then you must determine to be a firm parent. Parental consistency in the discipline of teens is vitally important in the formation of healthy character.

It is difficult for some parents to be firm, because they fear the disapproval of their teens. If you can't endure the temporary disapproval of your teens, then you lack the ability to be the kind of parent your teen desperately needs. Most of the time, your teens are happy to **have** you as their parents. You have to be tough enough to endure **those** times when you wouldn't win the election, if they were voting on parents. That will all change in a few years.

SUPERVISE YOUR TEENS. Remember what was said in an earlier chapter: Nothing can substitute for the responsible adult supervision of teenagers. Your opportunities for supervision are greater when you plan certain areas of your home to meet the social needs of your teens.

Dolores and I have always had room in our home for our youngsters. In their early teens, we furnished the recreation room for them and their friends. However, in their middle and later teens, they enjoyed the living room. It was set off from the rest of the house, so we could enjoy privacy with our friends, and they could have the same privilege. The room was attractively furnished and had the conveniences of draw drapes and nice stereo components, so our daughters enjoyed ending their dates there.

The wall on which the couch set was the same wall that framed the kitchen. Just on the other side of that wall sat the refrigerator. When our daughters and their dates would be sitting there on the couch listening to good music, my wife and I were aware of other activities that might have been preoccupying them. After all, it hadn't been that long since we sat on the couch in her parents' living room. Of course, we were good Christian young people, and so were our daughters and their dates. Nevertheless, we all know human nature—"that which is born of the flesh is flesh . . ." (John 3:6). So about every twenty minutes, I would go to the refrigerator. I would simply open the refrigerator door and close it. Then I would go back into the family room or bedroom. Of course I would never have embarrassed our children by going into the living room. However, neither they nor their dates knew that.

I remember one time, our oldest daughter said, "Dad, when my boyfriend and I are sitting on the couch listening to music in the living room, why do you go to the refrigerator so often? Don't you trust us?"

I thought a moment and said, "No, honey, I guess I don't trust you. I trust you with the family car, even with family credit cards, but in a dimly lit room, listening to soft music with a handsome young man and nothing else to entertain you but yourselves—no, under those circumstances I guess I don't completely trust you yet. But don't feel too bad, because I wouldn't trust myself with any other woman but your mother in circumstances like that."

She laughed, and I laughed. We both knew that during this transition from adolescence to adulthood teens need responsible adult supervision. This kind of loving nonpossessive concern helps them learn how to manage their increasing freedom more maturely.

GROUNDING CAN BE HELPFUL. Grounding, if it is applied by the event, can still be an effective way of enforcing limits with teenagers. Some parents try to ground teenagers over periods of time. When their youngsters disobey, they say, "You can't go anywhere for a month."

What thirteen-year-old or fifteen-year-old is going to behave for a whole month? So by the time the month goes by, the teen may have accumulated enough other offenses to ground him or her for the next three months. Grounding by time seldom proves to be an effective tool for the punishment of teenagers.

Grounding by event can be a very effective way of controlling teens. When your youngsters defy you or are disobedient or disrespectful to you, ground them for some event they have scheduled. Often simply threatening to do that will bring about the change of behavior you want. However, if you don't get the cooperation you want, exercise the grounding.

By refusing to let them stay all night with their friends, go to the ball game, or buy the special clothes they wanted, you may incur their wrath. If so, remind them that it is *their* behavior that has resulted in this unpleasantness for them—not *yours!*

This method of punishment also allows you to be merciful if you choose. If the event you're taking from your teen is particularly important and you want to extend mercy, you can give the teen a way to work off the grounding. Tasks assigned for working off groundings should not be those included in their usual responsibilities. Something extra should be required. This is a good way to get the basement cleaned, closets organized, the car waxed, and special yard work done. This approach exacts a penalty from the teen for his or her misbehavior. The parent is also given the option of being merciful without feeling as though he or she is being manipulated by the youngster's pleas.

CAR CONTROL HELPS. Control of the family car can also give you some real leverage with teens. Young people should learn that when they cooperate with Mom and Dad the car keys are much more available to them than when they disobey.

Even if your teen has his or her own car, help is often needed in paying the car insurance, keeping the gas tank filled, and covering the cost of repairs. So when your teens cooperate with you, be as liberal as you can be in helping them with these expenses. However, when he or she becomes difficult to manage, show him or her how stingy you can become in these matters.

These methods of dealing with teens simply teach them how the spiritual law of sowing and reaping works in the practical affairs of our daily lives. If they are going to be successful in life, they must learn this lesson. You can teach your young people that more mercifully in the home than they will ever learn it in the world.

They will never have a teacher who loves them as much as you. They will never have a manager or supervisor who will care as much about their future as you care. That is why it is so important that you teach your teens that when they accept fair limits imposed on them by others and carry out reasonable responsibilities required of them by others that they get freedom and privileges. However, when they overstep the limits and fail to carry out their responsibilities, freedom is restricted and privileges are cancelled.

Be Friendly!

Here is where many parents struggle. They have difficulty being firm, unless they are also being angry. Any parent is likely to "lose his cool" with teens once in a while. No one is angelic enough to have supervision of a teenager for seven to ten years and "keep her cool" all the time. Your teens know that. They don't expect you to be perfect. However, the less frequently you lose your temper with them the better it is going to be for your relationships.

PARENTAL AUTHORITY CAN BE DESTRUCTIVE. Now here are some expressions of parental authority that can be very damaging to your relationships with your teens. First of all, *don't mix love and hostility*. This gives your young people the impression that when they obey, you love them, but when they disobey, you don't love them. They feel as though when they obey, you accept them, and when they disobey, you reject them.

Your teens need to know that whether they are obeying or disobeying, you love them just the same and that whether they are obeying or disobeying, you accept them. In moments of parental anger and hostility, this message gets lost. Developing the ability to be friendly and firm will enable you to blend love and punishment in a healthy way.

Also, avoid contrasting control and freedom. Some parents make it very clear to their teens that the parents are the bosses. Somehow they have to get that across several times every day. Other parents, who are very much in control of their teens, manage to create the feeling that their teens are moving more and more into control of their own lives. Those are the healthy parents.

Avoid coming across as an authoritarian parent. An authoritarian refuses to explain the rules. When their teens ask, "Dad, why do you have these rules? Why do I have to do this? Why do I have to do that?" The parent says, "Because I say so! That's why you have to do it. The fact that I say it is all the 'why' you need." This type of parenting breeds rebellion. Even kids who normally would not think of rebelling are likely to do so against an authoritarian parent.

The other extreme is just as bad—the overly permissive parent. Such parents are either too preoccupied with their own lives to care about what their children do, or they have adopted a laissez-faire approach to parenthood that leaves children too much on their own. In either event the results are disastrous for teens.

BE AN AUTHORITATIVE PARENT. The authoritative parent is most helpful to teens. What is an authoritative parent? This type of parent comes across to the teens as someone who loves them and knows what parenting teens is all about. These parents are confident in their ability as parents. They are not afraid of their children. They know how to enforce their limits in a friendly way.

Authoritative parents love their children. They are sure their experience in living has equipped them to know more about what is best for their teens than they do. But these parents don't profess to be right all the time. They know that although parents may not always be right, parents are always necessary for teens. They know teens need loving authority over them. As authoritative parents see their teens mature, they are happy to turn the control of their lives gradually over to them.

As teens begin to make more and more of the decisions that chart their future, it is essential for them to define God's vocational will for their lives. At times, this has been presented in such a mystical way in the church that teens have found very little help in making this crucial life decision. In the next chapter, I will be offering some biblical suggestions for making the vocational will of God practical for your teenagers.

Seven

What Will My Work Be?

———————◆———————

Your teens will spend more of their adult lives working than doing any other activity. That's God's will for them. Work is not part of the curse.

In Genesis 2:8, 15 Moses plainly states that the day God created Adam He had a job for him to do: "And the Lord God planted a garden eastward in Eden; and there he put the man whom he had formed. . . . And the Lord God took the man, and put him into the garden of Eden to dress it and to keep it."

A person needs to work in order to feel fulfilled. In John 5:17 Jesus clearly states that this is part of God's image in us, for there He says, "My Father worketh hitherto, and I work."

Women and Careers

Genesis 2:18 tells us that Eve was created as a helpmeet for Adam. Eve worked with Adam in dressing and keeping the garden, at least until the children came. Through their work, Adam and Eve made a significant impact on their world.

SOME BIBLE WOMEN WERE CAREER WOMEN. Today's Christian career woman is doing nothing more than Christian women in the past have done. For example, look at Solomon's description of the "virtuous woman."

> She buys imported foods, brought by ship from distant ports. She gets up before dawn to prepare breakfast for her household, and plans the day's work for her servant girls. She goes out to inspect a field, and buys it; with her own hands she plants a vineyard. She is energetic, a hard worker, and watches for bargains. She works far into the night!
> She sews for the poor, and generously gives to the needy. She has no fear of winter for her household, for she has made warm clothes for all of them. She also upholsters with finest tapestry; her own clothing is beautifully made—a purple gown of pure linen. Her husband is well known, for he sits in the council chamber with the other civic leaders. She makes belted garments to sell to the merchants.
>
> Proverbs 31:14–24 TLB

This woman didn't neglect her children, but she obviously pursued a career other than homemaking.

Paul's first convert in Europe was a businesswoman. Here's how Luke describes her: "And a certain woman named Lydia, a seller of purple, of the city of Thyatira, which worshipped God, heard us: whose heart the Lord opened, that she attended unto the things which were spoken of Paul" (Acts 16:14).

In Acts 18:2,3 we're introduced to Aquila, whose wife Priscilla was a partner with him in their business of tentmaking. The casual way in which these women are mentioned in the New Testament indicates that it was not unusual for women to be engaged in these kinds of occupations.

YOUR DAUGHTER HAS A CHOICE. Make it easy for your daughter to discuss her career with you. Help her to sort out the advantages and disadvantages of a career in the home and compare them with those of a career out of the home.

At least 70 percent of married women work outside the home at sometime during their married life. The work they pursue is much more likely to be fulfilling if it is something they have anticipated and prepared for ahead of time. This kind of thought and planning needs to begin in junior-high school.

Choosing a Career

Work Can Be Fun

Much of our sense of fulfillment comes from our work and how we feel about it. Because of this, your view of work becomes a very important influence on the way you are emotionally affected by your work.

In the course of growing up, many youngsters develop a very unhealthy attitude toward work. They learn to see it as unenjoyable. Young people who fall into the habit of thinking this way are sentencing themselves to lives filled with an activity they have learned to dread.

God wants our work to be meaningful, but He also wants it to be fun. When believers feel they are doing the work God has called them to do and gifted them to do, they enjoy it most of the time. Adopting this kind of positive work attitude helps people find fulfillment in their work.

Career Choice Should Precede Mate Choice

In the Christian teen's priorities, career choice should precede mate choice. As you know, this seldom happens. Why? Even a casual look at our society reveals how sexually overstimulated it is—seductive advertising, suggestive lyrics in music, promiscuous plots on movie and television screens, and permissive attitudes toward pornography are prevalent. In this kind of an environment, how can we expect the average young person to concentrate on his or her career choice?

In most cases young people who are going to prepare for a career have to delay sexual gratification longer than those who get a job and go to work immediately after graduating from high school. So, unconsciously, the desire to escape sexual frustration often propels young people into thinking about marriage before they have seriously tried to discover how God has gifted them or where His vocational will may be for them.

Subsequently many young people take jobs that do not challenge them and bring them to their potential. Once they are married and have families, it is unlikely that they will ever have the opportunity to discover God's vocational best for their lives. Often their work becomes the boring and frustrating way they pay the expenses of their families. They receive little if any fulfillment or sense of dignity from what they are doing. What a loss!

Both the home and the church need to place much more emphasis on career choice. Helping teens gain a sense of vocational direction as early as possible in life provides them with some worthwhile goals toward which their sexual energies can be directed. Achieving these goals will provide them with a much more fulfilling and satisfying future.

Other Reasons Career Choice Is Important

Our stewardship of God's vocational gifts comprises our greatest responsibility before God. In Romans 12:3–8, Paul challenges us to determine what those gifts are. He admonishes us to develop them in service to God and man as a reasonable response to His mercies.

> For I say, through the grace given unto me, to every man that is among you, not to think of himself more highly than he ought to think; but to think soberly, according as God hath dealt to every man the measure of faith. For as we have many members in one body, and all members have not the same office: So we, being many, are one body in Christ, and every one members one of another. Having then gifts differing ac-

cording to the grace that is given to us, whether prophecy, let us prophesy according to the proportion of faith; Or ministry, let us wait on our ministering: or he that teacheth, on teaching; Or he that exhorteth, on exhortation: he that giveth, let him do it with simplicity; he that ruleth, with diligence; he that sheweth mercy, with cheerfulness.

Notice the practicality of Paul's instruction. He advises us not to think that we have certain gifts that we don't have, but to take a look at the gifts we do have. He urges us to consider them as God's unique way of equipping us to serve Him in the body of Christ—and in our vocational world.

MAXIMIZES INFLUENCE AND INCOME. Your teens need to know that God holds each of us responsible for the discovery and development of the vocational gifts He has given us. By defining those gifts and developing them, we maximize our impact upon our world.

In most cases, realizing God's vocational gifts will also maximize your teen's lifetime income. His or her lifetime earnings could be increased as much as a $.25 million to $.5 million. Think about what that will mean for your teen and for the kingdom of God.

Helping Christian young people determine God's will in their career choices is still an undiscovered field of ministry in many churches—and in many families. However, this ministry has tremendous potential.

I want to excite you about the possibilities of turning your young people on to their vocational potentials. Make them curious about their talents and abilities. Motivate them to discover and develop their gifts. Seeing them reap the benefits will more than compensate you for your efforts.

ALL GOD'S CHILDREN ARE GIFTED AND CALLED! The religious tradition in which I was raised prepared me well for the coming of the Lord and my death, but it did very little to help me find God's vocational will for my life. In fact, if a young person wasn't called to be a minister or missionary, he or she was left feeling that other vocational choices mattered very little.

The ministry is an honorable profession. Young people should be encouraged to pursue it. However, if God has gifted and called a young man or woman to another vocation, he or she should feel no less divinely directed. After all, the Bible introduces us to a variety of other occupations among its characters. Here are just a few found in the New Testament: coppersmith, physician, shepherd, saleswoman, lawyer, fisherman, tent maker, teacher, silversmith, sailor, soldier, tax collector.

The greatest satisfaction in life comes from knowing God's will and doing it—regardless of the vocation involved. Nothing dignifies life more than feeling you are providentially directed in pursuing your work. Every member of the body of Christ is entitled to this vocational affirmation.

Relating their faith to their work makes the will of God practical for young men and young women. For them, doing God's will has just as much to do with going to work as it does with going to church.

YOUR WORK CAN BE YOUR MINISTRY. Many Christians believe they work so they can support other people who are called to do God's will. Your teens need to know that their work *is* God's will for them. The people with whom they work are the mission field to which God has called them. They are to represent the Lord in their workaday world.

The excellent quality of their work and the enthusiasm they bring to the job are important aspects of their witness. For the wise worker, these qualities will open up many opportunities to influence people for the Lord. They will also increase chances for advancement on the job.

How Does a Young Person Find God's Vocational Will?

The will of God is both practical and mystical. Although God's will in many aspects of life remains a mystery, the Holy Spirit assures believers in Romans 12:2 that the will of God concerning their life work is practical enough to be proven: "And be not conformed to this world: but be ye transformed by the renewing of your mind, that ye may prove what is that good, and acceptable, and perfect, will of God."

God always calls people to do something that needs to be done. He always calls them to do what He has given them the ability to do. Some of our abilities are innate. However most of them are learned from the opportunities our environment provides us. Once a young person discovers what he or she can do well and has found areas where these skills are needed, a big step has been taken toward discovering God's will.

God's Highest Call Is Into the Body of Christ

We received God's highest call when the Holy Spirit called us into the body of Christ through the gospel. Every believer is a partaker of this high calling (Philippians 3:14).

Our heavenly Father sees each of His children as being of equal worth. He paid no more for one of us than He did for any of the others. Our roles in the kingdom are different, but each of us is of equal value to God.

The nature of our call has nothing to do with our worth to God. Whether we are called to be preachers, missionaries, truck drivers, masons, politicians, nurses, lawyers, or doctors, we are all equally loved by God. Each believer is to enjoy the importance of feeling called to whatever work he or she pursues.

Of course, the ministry gifts of Christ to the church are special. Paul reminds us in Ephesians 4:11: "And he [Christ] gave some, apostles; and some, prophets; and some, evangelists; and some, pastors and teachers." Their task is to train believers to do the work of the ministry. Since they are over us in the Lord, they are to be honored and respected for their work's sake. However, their callings are no higher than the calling of any other member in the body of Christ. After all, the highest calling of God is into the body of Christ— and every believer has responded to that call.

So after a person has obeyed the gospel, the important issue becomes finding his or her place in the body of Christ. In 1 Corinthians 12:12–20, Paul makes this point crystal clear:

For as the body is one, and hath many members, and all the members of that one body, being many, are one body: so also is Christ. For by one Spirit are we all baptized into one body, whether we be Jews or Gentiles, whether we be bond or free; and have been all made to drink into one Spirit. For the body is not one member, but many. If the foot shall say, Because I am not the hand, I am not of the body; is it therefore not of the body? And if the ear shall say, Because I am not the eye, I am not of the body; is it therefore not of the body? If the whole body were an eye, where were the hearing? If the whole were hearing, where were the smelling? But now hath God set the members every one of them in the body, as it hath pleased him. And if they were all one member, where were the body? But now are they many members, yet but one body.

How Can Teens Be Helped to Find God's Will?

Help your teen understand that people tend to view themselves in terms of their work. They identify themselves with their occupational titles. For example, if you ask a woman what she does, she may reply, "Oh, I'm just a housewife." Her reply implies that she doesn't attach much importance to what she does. If you do not attach much value to what you do, it is easy to begin thinking of yourself as unimportant. That is why I never let a woman tell me she is "just a housewife" without challenging her. I point out to her that she is certainly not the wife of any house. She is the wife of her husband. If she has chosen to limit her work within the home, she is a keeper of the home. This is a high and legitimate calling in itself. Such a woman is not "just a housewife"; she is a homemaker. At a time in our society when so many homes are breaking up, a woman who thinks of herself as a *homemaker* is bound to feel a greater sense of dignity in what she is doing than if she thought of herself merely as a *housewife*.

Other people will say, "I'm a medical assistant," "I'm a dental technician," "I'm a doctor," "I'm a nurse," "I'm a secretary," or, "I'm an engineer." The kind of work you do and the way you view it says a lot about the dignity you attribute to your life. This is why it is important for your teen to see that a person usually attaches more dignity to work he or she has chosen than to a job he or she has to do in order to pay life's expenses. If young people do not prepare for a chosen task in life, then one less desirable will most likely be forced upon them.

WHEN SHOULD PREPARATION BEGIN? By the time your teens enter junior-high school, they should be knowledgeable about the job market and thinking seriously about where they fit in it. By the time your youngster is through high school, he or she should have developed a saleable skill that is in demand in the marketplace.

MARKETABLE SKILLS ARE NECESSARY! I never will forget how my wife had to badger our younger daughter to take typing. She didn't want to take typing. She argued, "But Mother, I'm not going to be a secretary. I'm going to be a professional woman. Other people will do my typing."

Then her mother wisely reminded her, "Honey, you will need to work while you are getting your education. Typing skills will help you get the jobs you need to pay your way through school." Today my daughter is an attorney but the typing skills she didn't want to learn were what helped to pay her way through college. Needless to say, she has thanked her mother many times for insisting that she acquire them.

As a parent, you must see that your teens become sensitive to the job market early in junior-high school. Insist on their acquiring some marketable skills before they get out of high school. To be out of school and unprepared for work is tragic.

Four Different Career Patterns

Career patterns extending over a person's life will vary with the nature of the person and the nature of his or her vocational choice. By becoming familiar with several career patterns, parents are better prepared to help their teens discover the direction they need.

1. STABLE CAREER PATTERNS. Professional careers generally follow a stable pattern. If your son or daughter is to be a physician or

an engineer, that decision must be made very early in life because of the extended period of preparation required. It is highly unlikely that a person who has invested so much time in preparation for a career will change job tracks later in life. That is why the career pattern of a professional person is so predictable and stable.

2. CONVENTIONAL CAREER PATTERNS. In a conventional career pattern, young persons prepare to work in a business or factory. They may feel inclined toward management or production. However, they begin at the job entry level their skills have prepared them for and work toward the rewards and promotions afforded by their employer.

3. UNSTABLE CAREER PATTERNS. Some job and career patterns are unstable. Artists and musicians face this fate. They experience feast and famine in their work. This tests the patience of parents. Family support is critical in helping talented musicians and artists find their way. Thank God for the opportunities afforded this group of gifted young people in Christian media ministries.

4. MULTIPLE TRIAL CAREER PATTERNS. Some young people discover God's vocational will through multiple job trials. That is, they will have several jobs in their twenties and perhaps not find the stable job they want until they are in their early thirties.

How Is God's Vocational Will Discovered?

Understanding these various routes to vocational maturity can help parents be more confident in providing the support and guidance their young people need during the search. Remember, a positive self-image and accurate self-knowledge are essential to a healthy vocational choice.

In Romans 12:6–8, Paul lists seven gifts, which are abilities or aptitudes to be developed and used in ministry to the body of Christ. He instructs his readers to discover, by trial and error, which gifts from among these represent God's good, acceptable, and perfect will for them. Your teens can use this same practical, biblical strategy in discovering the natural abilities and talents God has given them.

Information obtained from aptitude and interest tests give valuable clues as to where your teens' gifts lie. Intelligence tests will indicate their ability to successfully attempt any training necessary for reaching their goals. Manual dexterity tests are available for assessing the skills of those interested in trades. The *Dictionary of Occupational Titles,* found in school libraries or the public library, informs young people of the earning opportunities and potential job demand for hundreds of occupations. Junior and senior high school counselors will be glad to assist your teens in their search.

Young people need encouragement in discovering their talents and abilities. Reassure them that God's vocational will is practical. It is to be found among the things that need to be done, among the things they can do well, and among the things they enjoy doing.

Challenge your teens to investigate a broad field of vocational possibilities before determining their final direction. Assure them that God will confirm His will by giving them confidence and success in pursuit of their goals.

Focusing their gifts and abilities on well-defined vocational goals can lessen your teens' frustrations in life. By helping your teens discover their abilities and develop their goals, you are enabling them to constructively channel energies that could otherwise fuel destructive teenage rebellion.

Eight

Getting the Best of Rebellion

———◆———

Launching teens into life places more stress on parents than all other demands of parenting combined. Through all those years, as your children are striving to become adults, you feel as if your parenthood is on the line. You can't physically control your children any longer, but what they do continues to honor or humiliate you and the family. The decisions they make seriously affect their futures—and yours as well.

Because of the anxiety parenting teenagers generates, some parents fail to realize that their teens are also caught up in a whirlwind of conflict, frustration, and confusion. This is why some people refer to adolescence as the "salad" age: the time in life when young people are green, mixed up, and full of vinegar.

TEEN YEARS ARE FILLED WITH TENSION! Adolescents are too old to be considered children and too young to be treated as adults. Frequently they feel caught between their parents and their peers. They want to please both, but when they can't, the peers frequently win.

During this stormy period, parents and teens frighten and anger each other. Typically parents fear youngsters will make some impulsive decisions that will tragically complicate their futures. The common areas of concern are reckless driving, abuse of drugs, and sexual misbehavior. Parents become upset when their teens violate reasonable limits that have been set to protect them from these risks.

Of course, young people seldom agree that the rules set by their parents are reasonable. They are fearful that their parents will never let them grow up and are frustrated by the limited freedom they have.

These are simply the normal tensions most parents and their teens experience in the tug-of-war between them during the teen's transition into adult life. Parents need to know the difference between this normal state of affairs and adolescent rebellion.

What Is Adolescent Rebellion?

Let me give you a definition of adolescent rebellion that will help you know it when you see it: "Adolescent rebellion is the persistent and flagrant disregard of authority in the wanton and deliberate pursuit of the teenager's own interests."

This definition makes it obvious that most parents deal with healthy teens who are engaging in the normal struggle for their independence. Every generation of parents and teens has its share of confrontations in determining how much freedom the teens should have and what responsibilities they should be expected to assume. Usually teens want more freedom than parents are willing to give, and parents want to assign more responsibility than teens want to assume.

However, you will be glad to know that 80 percent of our teens deal with the tension of this struggle without resorting to rebellion. Only about 20 percent choose to get into their own worlds by rebelling against their parents.

When rebellion does occur, it can be very painful for parents and horribly destructive for teenagers. So if you and your teen must endure the agony of rebellion, let me explain some of the dynamics involved in your struggles and make some practical suggestions for dealing with them.

Parental Dynamics

Before we focus on what is happening within the adolescent who chooses to rebel, let's take a look at what is going on in the lives of parents while they are launching their teens into adulthood. During these years, parents are experiencing their own midlife stresses.

First of all, evidences of aging are inescapable. A look in the mirror reminds middle-aged parents of how many times they have been around the sun. Gravity is taking its toll. Men are displaying all the Bs of midlife—baldness, bifocals, brown spots, bulges, and bunions. Women are going through menopause.

MIDLIFE MADNESS! During their forties and fifties, some men and women nearly panic over the loss of their youth. As a couple sees their teenagers begin to date, they are reminded of their own younger days.

If they married when they were very young, seeing the liberty their teenagers enjoy may remind them of the freedom early marriage cost them. In some middle-aged people, such a reminder can trigger off an irrational urge to recover that lost adolescent love time. Such an urge, coupled with a fear of aging, is what sparks many midlife affairs. That's why these two decades of life are sometimes referred to as the "philandering forties and fifties."

A husband's affair during this time of life is particularly devastating to his wife, especially if she concludes from the affair that she is no longer attractive to her husband because she is no longer young. In most cases, the husband's affair has nothing to do with his wife's aging. More likely, he is acting out of his own fear of aging.

DEPRESSION FROM EARLY MEMORIES. Second, if parents have unpleasant memories from their teens, they may unconsciously surface during these years and become painful sources of anxiety, hostility, and depression. Should this be the case, the parent in volved needs to seek the help of a competent Christian counselor in dealing with these feelings. Significant healing can result.

PARENTS ARE LIKELY TO SUFFER MAJOR ILLNESSES. As though this were not enough, your parents are likely to experience major health breaks during the years when you are raising your teens. After all, most of us bury our parents during our forties and fifties. So often while we are launching our teenagers into life and dealing with the anxiety of our own aging, we are also confronted with our parents' deaths.

FINANCIAL STRESS PEAKS. Fourth, family expenses peak during these years. When our children are small, we sometimes complain about the pediatrician's bills and the costs of infant care. However, once we learn what it costs to feed and clothe adolescents, we realize how relatively inexpensive babies are. Since many teens are unable to find work, financing their social life adds additional pressure to the family budget.

ESCAPE IS NOT THE ANSWER! If a couple has not built a strong and healthy marriage, the husband finds it easy to escape into his work more and more, while the wife may tend to cling to the children. This way, neither of them have to come to terms with the painful issues between them.

When the children are launched into life, the bubble breaks. Mother realizes she no longer has her children and the tasks of parenthood to give meaning to her life. Father knows the children will no longer function as a cushion between him and his wife. The fact that they are going to be alone dawns on them both.

For many marriages, divorce becomes a real threat at this time. In fact, if you took a look at our divorce statistics, you would find one of the sharpest peaks occurs during the forties and the fifties.

Now you can see more clearly why the forties and fifties are often referred to as the most stressful years of life.

Teen Dynamics

Teenage rebellion is not necessarily related to your parenting skills. Although overly controlling and overly permissive parents predispose their teens to rebel, very competent parents may also have a teen who rebels. Parents can be loving and fair in their discipline but if the teenager doesn't see himself or herself being treated fairly, he or she may rebel.

After all, it is not the facts of our lives that we live with. We live with our *perception* of the facts of our lives. Parents may be able to control the ways they choose to act toward their children, but they cannot control the way their children choose to perceive their actions. Often it is the teens' perceptions of the way they are treated, not the treatment itself, that triggers off rebellion.

TEENS EXPERIENCE STRONG SEXUAL AND AGGRESSIVE URGES. Remember, upon entering adolescence, teenagers are rapidly approaching physiological maturity. They are experiencing strong surges of sexual and aggressive energy. Many teens are as large or larger than their parents. Even though they are still economically dependent upon their parents, they want to assert their independence.

In determining to be his or her own person, a teen wants the freedom to try out value systems different from the family's. This is very frightening to most parents. They fear the teen will use this new freedom to become so different from the family that they will be strangers to each other for the rest of their lives. At the same time, the teen fears, *If I become the kind of person my mom and dad want me to be, I will be so much like them I won't know who I am.*

A careful look at each generation proves how exaggerated these fears of both parents and teens are. A careful observation of young adults reveals that very few teenagers break completely away from their parents' values. This should be comforting to anxious parents. Observing the differences between each new generation of young adults and their parents should be equally comforting for teenagers.

WHAT WERE YOU LIKE AS A TEENAGER? As a parent, go back and think of the things you did when you were a teen. Didn't you try some things that were outside the boundaries of your family's faith? When you were caught, do you remember how painful the clash was between you and your parents? Do you remember the days and nights of tension between you?

Nevertheless, the love you and your parents shared with each other didn't let you get too far apart. No doubt you tested your parents' limits. Most likely you finally resolved the tension between you and them by changing enough to become your own person but at the same time, adopting values near enough to your family's values to allow the family to get along well and continue life together. In all probability the tension between you and your teens will be resolved in a similar way.

Some Directions for Managing Teenage Rebellion

Unfortunately some parents are confronted by rebellious teens. This is a very unpleasant scene for the teen and for the parent. If you are forced to face such a painful ordeal, here are some suggestions for managing it as well as possible.

DON'T PANIC! Remember Solomon's promise, "Train up a child in the way he should go: and when he is old, he will not depart from it" (Proverbs 22:6). Notice, Solomon did not say he would *never* depart from it. He simply said "when he is old" he will not depart from it.

You see, permanent parental satisfaction is a long-term goal. Between childhood and maturity are many hair-raising moments when you think your teen will never make it. At times you will think the distance that's growing between you and your son or daughter is so great that in spite of all you and your teen can do, you will never be able to bridge it.

Let me reassure you—except in rare instances—that distance will be bridged! That is why my first advice to parents who must manage teen rebellion is—*don't panic*. Panic never helps resolve the rebellion, it only makes it worse.

DON'T PREACH! Do you remember how "fascinated" you were by your parents' preaching when you were a teenager? Do you remember how much good their sermons did you? Very few young people are revolutionized by sermons their parents preach. Young people don't respond very well to preaching parents.

However, young people are very bright. If you have something to say, say it. They may not agree with you, but you need to say what is on your mind in a forceful and respectful way, and they need to hear it.

Once you have said what you want to say with conviction, then assume your teen understands your strong feelings in the matter. Saying it again and again, more heatedly each time, will seldom if ever be effective in changing the behavior of teens for the better. In fact, such an exchange usually only intensifies their determination to rebel.

Don't try to force your faith on your teenager. Often parents struggle with the question of how long they should make their teen go to church with them. My suggestion is to require your youngsters to go to church as long as the law requires them to go to school. This is not a perfect rule, but it is a defendable one.

DON'T NAG! Nagging is a most ineffective way of changing behavior. So as best you can, avoid hostile and demanding statements such as, "As long as you are under my roof, you will do as I say," or, "When are you going to learn to come home when you are supposed to?" You only harm the relationship you have with your teens when you nag like this.

If your teens have overstepped the limits, then we have covered in previous chapters what you should do: The teens forfeit their privileges. You don't take their *rights* away from them, but remember, if they haven't earned their *privileges,* they shouldn't get them. You don't ground them for a month, but you do take an event away from them that they desire to participate in very much. This is far better than nagging.

DON'T ABDICATE! Some parents believe they can end their teens' rebellion by giving in to their demands. Nothing could be farther from the truth.

If teens are going to rebel, they need consistent parents to rebel against. If parents relax the limits every time teens rebel against them, then you can expect teens to rebel against these changed limits. If teens are going to rebel, parents should given them good, firm, consistent limits to rebel against.

What If Your Teen Runs Away?

Some parents are fearful that any firmness at all may result in their teenager running away from home. Only in rare cases does this kind of loving firmness result in such an action. Teens often threaten to run away, but they seldom do.

If your teen *does* run away, how should you respond? Age is a factor that has to be taken into consideration when dealing with this kind of family crisis.

If your youngster is thirteen or fourteen years of age, you will probably find more help from your local police in trying to locate him or her. It is more difficult for most youngsters this age to pass themselves off as young adults. Generally they are more dependent and less capable of taking care of themselves. So usually in two or three days, their protest is over, and they want to come home.

Young people in their middle teens are more streetwise and harder to detect among young adults. When they decide to run away from home, they are extremely difficult for police officers to identify. Of course the police should be notified, and a missing-person report should be filed. However unless the family can afford a private detective, it is unlikely that much will be done to locate these youngsters until they are ready to contact the family.

Our police departments are overwhelmed with too many more serious crimes, and youngsters can evade police detection in too many ways for domestic problems like this to be placed very high on law enforcement's agenda. So unless there is evidence of foul play in a young person's disappearance, the family will be largely on their own in attempting to find their child.

DON'T SHOOT GNATS WITH CANNONS! When I hear the insignificant issues that get blown out of all reasonable proportion in parent-teen confrontations, it saddens me. Several years ago, late one night,

I arrived in South Carolina for a speaking engagement. Almost everything in town was closed, and I was hungry. I approached a cab driver and asked if he could find me a place to get a hamburger.

On the way to the diner, we started to talk. He wanted to know about my work, so I told him I was a minister and a psychologist. With that information, he began to open up. "I wish I could have talked to you just twenty-four hours earlier," he said. "I had a run-in with my son over the length of his hair. I told him if he didn't cut his hair he could get out of my house."

By this time, tears were in the cabbie's eyes. "My boy left last night, and I don't know what to do. He was just sixteen."

I told him to inquire at his son's friends' homes. I also encouraged him to visit the places he knew his son hung around. We usually advise parents to do these things when their teens run away.

By this time, we were at the diner. I had a brief word of prayer with him. I asked God to help him in his search for his son and to help them reconcile their differences.

As I got out of the cab he said, "Believe me, if I had it to do over again, I wouldn't chase my kid away from home because of the length of his hair."

MAKE A NEW START. Usually, youngsters in the early and middle teens will only run away once. After they have been away for a few days, home has never looked so good to them.

Be wise enough to treat your teen's return home like a new start in your relationship with him or her. If you have made some mistakes in the heat of managing the crisis, admit them. Most young people are more than willing to forgive their parents and offer their own apologies. You will need to apply some sanctions, but make them merciful enough to be consistent with your desire to reconcile your relationship with your teen. However you may have to require the youngster to stay home until enough self-discipline is learned for you to feel comfortable in granting him or her liberty again.

Talk to your teen about the issues that led to his or her running away. Remember, this has not been a pleasant experience for your teen. The pain of acting so impulsively can also be counted on to discipline him or her in the future. Usually the anxiety and emotional pain of such an experience drastically reduce the likelihood of your teen running away again.

YOUNGSTERS DETERMINED TO RUN AWAY CAN'T BE STOPPED. Although parents want to do everything they can to keep their teens from the frightening risks of running away, some youngsters won't let you protect them. Some teens are determined to run away from home.

When this is the case, you can do little about it, especially if your teen is out of high school and in a state of rebellion. So don't deceive yourself into thinking you can keep your teen at home by allowing your teen whatever he or she wants. Reasonable limits are necessary. Abandoning them will only make a bad situation worse.

SOMETIMES PEACEFUL SEPARATION IS THE BEST ANSWER. Older young people may adopt a life-style that is so different from the parents that they should be separated from the family. For example, if you have an eighteen-year-old or nineteen-year-old youngster who is regularly smoking marijuana or using other drugs and maybe even dealing in them, you should seriously consider lovingly separating this teen from the family. Separation is particularly important if you still have younger children in the home.

Parents should be united in this action. The father should take the initiative in approaching the son or daughter. Advance notice should be given so the teen can have an opportunity to reconsider his or her behavior.

Once you and your teen agree that peaceful separation is better for everyone than continuing to battle each other, the three of you should look for a place for the teenager to live. If possible, you should furnish the first two or three months' rent for the youngster. However, it should be clearly understood that after that, he or she will be responsible for living expenses. Let your teen know that he or she will be welcome home for a meal or an evening together once in a while.

THE STRUGGLE FOR VALUES IS HEALTHY. Allow your teen the privacy of his or her own struggle for values. By this time you should have provided the spiritual, social, and sexual guidelines that you believe to be healthy. That's all God holds you responsible for.

Remember how important your own spiritual struggle was to you, and allow your teen the right to his or her own struggle. Commit your teen to the Lord. After all, He can speak when you have to be silent. Pray for your teen. However don't forget to pray also for yourself: Your having a nervous breakdown is not going to help your teenager.

COME TO TERMS WITH POWERLESSNESS AND HELPLESSNESS. One of the most difficult things parents have to face in coming to terms with teen rebellion is their powerlessness and helplessness. When your children are physically smaller than you are, you can protect them from dangers their immaturity and lack of judgment would expose them to. When your teen is bent on rebellion, you reach a point where you simply cannot do anything about it.

The sooner you can recognize this and accept your powerlessness and your helplessness, the more wisely you are likely to manage the situation. This is frightening! To try and reach out to protect a teenager bent on rebellion usually only intensifies the teen's need to rebel. Parents of rebellious teenagers have to love them enough to let them go.

This is the kind of unconditional love God has for us as His children. Even though God may not approve of what I do, He loves me just the same. God can help the parents of rebellious teens to love them for who they are, in spite of what they do.

Keep your communication with your teen. Listen to your teen's point of view. You don't have to agree, but at least listen. This is enough to satisfy many teens, they just want a hearing.

Be patient with yourself! Remember, it is difficult to love your teen when he or she is making you look like such a failure as a parent. However, you can learn to love your teen with the love of the Lord.

AGAPE LOVE WILL SEE YOU THROUGH! The love of the Lord will help you love your youngsters regardless of what they do. You may detest what they do, but you can still love them.

We went through some painful days of rebellion with our son. He is the only one of our children who had any serious difficulty moving through the teens into adulthood.

I remember being stretched out on the floor one day, just crying and praying about him. The Holy Spirit abruptly interrupted my prayer and spoke these words to my heart, "Now how much of your crying and praying is for your son and how much of it is for your concern about the effect of his behavior on your reputation as a parent?"

An honest answer to this question is difficult for most parents to determine. Believe me, just thinking about the question dried my tears up in a hurry. I realized that most of my pain was brought on by anger over my powerlessness to do anything about a situation that I considered embarrassing as a parent and threatening to my son.

Once the Lord helped me admit my own powerlessness and helplessness, I reached out to my son in His love. Of course, as I began to build my side of the bridge, my son began to build his side. It wasn't long until the distance between us disappeared and reconciliation restored the joy of our family love.

Remember, 80 percent of our teens are going to make it into adulthood without resorting to rebellion. Only 20 percent of young people are going to need the kind of help we have been talking about in this chapter.

Don't allow the devil to make you think that the heartbreaking chapter your teenager may be writing in the book of his or her life now is the end of the story. There will be other heart-lifting chapters. Distances will be bridged. Music and joy will return to your home.

Remember the story of the prodigal son in the fifteenth chapter of

Luke's gospel? Jesus did not say the boy's father had failed in raising him. Nor did he say the boy was bad. He simply made the point
that some children have to get a long way from home before they
realize how good they had it there and how great their parents are.

Thank God, adolescence is one of those transient experiences of
life that can be described with that four-word New Testament phrase
". . . it came to pass." As a parent, aren't you glad it doesn't come to
stay?

Part IV
Helping Your Teens Choose Companions in Life

Nine

Healthy Friendships Are Important

———————◆———————

Love from which friendships are built has its roots in the family. In fact, your first friends should be members of your own family. As you love your children and teach them to love each other you are providing them with the basic skills for building friendships.

By maintaining healthy friendships with other adults, you are modeling friendship skills for your teens. They overhear your telephone conversations with your friends. They watch your relationships in after-church social times and on other occasions. Through such informal and spontaneous ways, you are teaching your teens how to make friends.

Friendship Skills Are Learned

Personal warmth and hospitality are great assets in building friendships. For the most part, these are acquired characteristics.

Hypothetically speaking, anyone can learn them. However, your teens are more likely to be warm and hospitable if they observe these qualities in you. As you bring your friends into your home and take your teenagers into theirs, you are providing your teens valuable opportunities for learning friendship skills.

Just think, by something as simple as entertaining friends in your home eight or ten times a year, you can help your children learn how to be comfortable with others.

On the other hand, if your parents did not help you learn how to build friendships, you may feel so uncomfortable around people that you socialize very little. In that case, you are unwittingly passing on to your children the same kind of social awkwardness you inherited from your parents.

Healthy Christians Are Hospitable

Remember, healthy Christians are hospitable. They share their home with their friends. This is the way the early church evangelized.

> And they, continuing daily with one accord in the temple, and breaking bread from house to house, did eat their meat with gladness and singleness of heart, Praising God, and having favour with all the people. And the Lord added to the church daily such as should be saved.
>
> Acts 2:46, 47

If you are not already practicing this Christian grace of hospitality, why not start? Such an expression of practical Christian love will enrich your life and help your teenagers learn invaluable social skills.

Friends Are Important to Your Teens

Friends are a vital part of your teens' futures. Sooner or later, they will need your help in learning how to select their friends and build their friendships. The wiser and more nondirect you can be in providing this guidance, the more likely it is that your teens will accept it.

Consciously or unconsciously every teen has to learn to deal with such questions as: Where should I find my friends? Whom should I choose for my friends? How do I build a friendship? Let's look at each of these questions carefully.

Where Should Teens Find Their Friends?

Environment is an important factor in a person's choice of friends. If people voluntarily share a common environment, that environment must be meeting common needs for them.

For example, if teens choose their friends at a pot party, pot parties must be meeting certain needs for them and their friends. How healthy and constructive can friendships be when they are formed in such an illegal and irresponsible environment?

What are some of the safest environments in which your teens may find friends? Normally, your neighborhood, your teens' school, and your church would be safe places for finding friends. Friendships formed in these places are visible to parents and are rather easily monitored. However, these environments are not risk free. That is why it is so important for you to know your teens' friends and to wisely supervise their friendships.

Various Kinds of Friends

Teach your teen to appreciate several kinds of friends. For example, here are four different levels of friendships most teens will experience:

CASUAL FRIENDS. These are people that we often see in our daily activities, but only get to know in superficial ways. Each of us has many casual friends. Passing the time of day with them is pleasant, but that is all we share.

RECREATIONAL FRIENDS. These are people that we meet for fun and games. However, when the recreation we share with them is over, we part company until we meet to play again.

ACADEMIC FRIENDS. These are people they study with. They help each other prepare for exams, but when school is over, they seldom see each other.

CLOSE FRIENDS. Each of us needs two or three *close friends*. These friendships help us get through the rough times of life with less pain and celebrate the good times with more joy. These are the people we think of calling first when we are hurting or when we have good news to share.

In early adolescence, our close friends are likely to be members of the same sex. However, in middle and late adolescence, they may include both members of our own sex and those of the opposite sex.

Choosing Friends

CLOSE FRIENDS SHOULD BE CHOSEN CAREFULLY. Our close friends have a powerful influence on our futures. That is why parents of young people in their early and middle teens should not allow friendships to form which are obviously unhealthy for their teens. Some parents learn this lesson too late.

Darin and Melanie were raising their first teenager, and they wanted to be less restrictive with her than their parents had been with them. Heather, their thirteen-year-old daughter, seemed to sense this.

While visiting her girl friend, Heather caught the eye of the girl's nineteen-year-old brother, Doug. Heather couldn't get him off her mind.

One night, when Heather was at her girl friend's, Doug asked her to go to a movie with him. Of course Heather pled with her mother and father to let her go.

Darin and Melanie should have nipped this relationship in the bud. They should never have permitted Heather to go. However Heather convinced them that nothing was wrong with her going to the movie with Doug and implied that if they didn't let her go, they were being cruel to her.

So wanting more than anything else to be "understanding" parents, they caved in to Heather's pressure. In effect they were allowing Heather to teach them how to parent her.

What was wrong with their permitting Heather to go with Doug? In the first place, if you let a thirteen-year-old girl begin to single date, what will she be doing when she is sixteen and seventeen? No thirteen-year-old girl is emotionally mature enough to manage such a potentially serious experience.

In addition, Doug was nineteen years old. This should have immediately raised the suspicions of prudent parents. Why should a nineteen-year-old young man be interested in a thirteen-year-old girl?

Heather's interest in Doug is easy to understand. A young teenage girl is flattered to think that she is woman enough to command the interest of a nineteen-year-old young man. However, only a very immature nineteen-year-old young man would allow himself to be attracted to a thirteen-year-old girl.

The concern is not over the number of years between their ages. If Doug were twenty-seven and Heather were twenty-one, the situation would be entirely different. However, a girl experiences tremendous growth and change in those years from thirteen to twenty-one.

Heather deserved the advantage that such growth and change would give her in evaluating Doug, but he was too immature to understand that. Unfortunately her parents did not insist on protecting her from her own immaturity.

For the first few times Doug and Heather were out together, he respected the curfew Heather's parents had set for her. However, one night, after they had gone together a few months, Heather didn't come home. Her parents were frantic.

Darin went to look for Doug and Heather. He found them at Doug's apartment.

By the time Darin reached the apartment, Heather was drunk. He insisted that she come home with him. Darin and Melanie had never seen their daughter in this condition. They were understandably brokenhearted. They were so angry at Doug for allowing Heather to get into this condition that they determined to break up his relationship with her. Heather was emotionally devastated and subsequently tried to take her own life.

In the months of therapy that followed, Heather came to grips with her grief over the loss of Doug. She successfully confronted her hostility and anger toward her parents. Today Heather and her parents have a better relationship than they have ever had.

Now after all the pain generated by her experience, Heather understands that thirteen-year-olds don't always know what is best for them. Darin and Melanie are less reluctant to superimpose their good judgment on their young teenager.

DON'T BE AFRAID TO BREAK UNHEALTHY FRIENDSHIPS! Wise parents don't let relationships like this get started with their permission. Trust your own judgment as to which of your teens' friendships are healthy and which are unhealthy. Once you determine a relationship is unhealthy, intervene without hesitation—break it up! Intervention of this kind needs to be made lovingly, but it must be made firmly!

Whenever possible, boost the self-image of your teenager. Remember, your teens' friends are a projection of the way they see themselves. Praise their choice of friends whenever you can. Don't forget, when you knock their friends, you are knocking them.

However, if you can't approve of a friendship, don't hesitate to forbid it, regardless of the temporary reaction of your teenager. If you know the friendship is not healthy, don't feel guilty for breaking it up.

TEENS REFLECT THEMSELVES IN THEIR CHOICE OF FRIENDS. If you have given your teens a good image of themselves, this will be reflected in the kinds of friends they choose most of the time. If your teens are choosing the kinds of friends that embarrass you, then you need to take a serious look at the way they feel about themselves. As you are successful in helping them change the way they see themselves this change will be reflected in their choices of more wholesome friends.

TEENS TRUST PEERS MORE THAN PARENTS. Early adolescents tend to trust their friends more than they trust their parents. The friends of middle adolescents have a more profound effect on their adolescents' values than do their parents. Late adolescents and young adults choose their mates from among their friends. That is why healthy friendships are so important to young people.

In 2 Corinthians 6:17, 18 Paul admonishes Christians to choose their close friends from among Christians: "Wherefore come out from among them, and be ye separate, saith the Lord, and touch not the unclean thing; and I will receive you, And will be a Father unto you, and ye shall be my sons and daughters, saith the Lord Almighty."

People who are not Christians can be included among the Christian's casual and recreational friends. However the Christians should find their close friends from among those who are committed to Jesus Christ.

How Teenagers Build Friendships

A person who is going to build healthy friendships must be comfortable with himself or herself. Teens who have difficulty making friends should take a look at how they feel about themselves. Self-comfort is a basic skill in building healthy friendships.

Until your teens are comfortable with themselves, they will have difficulty being comfortable around other people. Once they have learned to be comfortable with themselves, they can focus on helping other people to be comfortable with them.

Junior-high-schoolers find it easier to be comfortable with members of their own sex than with members of the opposite sex. However, high-schoolers also need to feel comfortable with members of the opposite sex if they are going to build healthy social lives for themselves.

PRACTICE MAKES PERFECT! Like any other skill, social skills improve with practice. The more often teenagers are around members of the opposite sex, the more comfortable they become with them.

Young teenagers, both males and females, tend to be frightened and anxious around members of the opposite sex. However, with parental encouragement and more opportunities for practice, these fears and anxieties gradually fade away.

LOYALTY IS AN ESSENTIAL FRIENDSHIP SKILL. If teenagers are going to build healthy friendships, they must learn to be loyal to their friends. This means that, except in rare circumstances, parents should not pressure teens to break the confidences of their friends. The refusal of one teen to tell on another is a healthy sign of loyalty.

Under what circumstances should teens be urged to reveal the confidences of their friends? If a friend is involved in a pregnancy or substance-abuse problems, their parents should know about it. Help your teens understand that no teenager should be left to deal with these problems alone. Sooner or later, parents need to know. The sooner they know, the more they can do to help their troubled teenager.

FRIENDS MUST BE ABLE TO LOVE UNSELFISHLY. Finally, if teens are going to build healthy friendships, they must be able to love unselfishly. No healthy friendship is one-sided. Healthy friendships know how to give as well as receive.

Five Ways to Attract Friends!

There are many young people who are willing to work hard at making friends but simply do not know what to do. Some parents who have no difficulty making friends of their own find it difficult to tell their teens how to do it, so here are some practical tips you can share with your teens when they need help in learning how to make friends.

1. LEARN TO MAKE OTHERS FEEL IMPORTANT. How do you go about doing that?

First of all, ask the person whose friendship you seek questions about events in his or her world. Most of us like to inform other people about our worlds. That's why we tend to like people who get us to talk about ourselves.

Compliment them freely. Don't flatter them. That is embarrassing. However, everyone likes compliments.

What is the difference between compliments and flattery? It's flattering to say to a young lady in front of her friends, "You are the prettiest girl in this room." This remark would probably make her uncomfortable. However, she would like to hear, "You look very attractive tonight."

Starting a "compliment club" in the home can do wonders for building good relations among parents and teens. Determining to give each person in the family at least one compliment each day soon makes complimenting others a habit. What a wonderful way to acquire such an important friendship skill!

2. DON'T BE PHONY! BE REAL! Avoid exaggerations of your own accomplishments. People don't like braggarts. Don't be afraid to admit your faults and fears. Other people will appreciate your transparency.

3. EXPRESS YOUR POSITIVE FEELINGS ABOUT PEOPLE. Teens often complain about being criticized more than praised. Be sure you are praising your teens more than criticizing them. Then you can help them learn the importance of seeing the good in others. Simply noticing the positive things in other people will win a person many friends.

Help your teens learn the importance of saying things to their friends like, "You're neat." "I like to be around you." "You're an interesting person." "You're a lot of fun." Notice, the word *love* wasn't mentioned. That should be a special word to be used sparingly with very special people. One of the reasons it tends to be overused is that young people simply don't know what else to say.

Incidentally, while we are talking about expressing positive feelings for people, be sure you are setting the example for your teens. Let this practice become contagious in the family. After all, you want to hear your teens express positive feelings about you, too. Don't you?

4. DO FAVORS FOR YOUR FRIENDS. This kind of unselfishness is rewarded in many ways. By taking the time to do things for your friends you demonstrate how highly you value their friendship.

5. DON'T BE POSSESSIVE! Be willing to share your friends with others. Your teens need to know that the more possessive we become of our friends, the fewer friends we will have. Do you remember the nursery rhyme about Peter the pumpkin eater?

> Peter, Peter, pumpkin eater,
> Had a wife and couldn't keep her.
> Put her in a pumpkin shell,
> And there he kept her very well.

A pumpkin shell is no place for a wife—or a friend!

Friendships Are Built in Stages

In addition to this kind of practical advice, explain to your teens that healthy friendships are built in stages. Here is an explanation of those stages to share with your teenagers.

1. BUILDING RAPPORT. The first time you are with someone, you get some idea about the chemistry of the relationship. After you have been together two or three times, if there is little or no rapport between you and even less chemistry, it is probably not wise for you to invest any more time or energy in your effort to build a friendship with that person.

The fact that two people don't share enough in common to build a friendship doesn't mean that there is anything wrong with either of them, nor does it mean that they are destined to be enemies. They are simply different! Each of them will be able to find many others with whom they share enough in common to build healthy and enjoyable friendships.

However, if the chemistry is right and the rapport begins to grow, then you may want to test the friendship further.

2. GETTING TO KNOW EACH OTHER. In this second stage of friendship building, you tell each other more about yourselves. This kind of sharing should be done mutually and equitably.

Often young women share more freely about themselves than do young men. In that event, early in the relationship, a young man may know his girl friend's entire family history while he remains a relative stranger to her. This is never healthy.

Teach your teenager the wisdom of testing a friend's ability to keep confidences by first sharing something that is personal, but not intimate enough to be damaging if it were told.

For example, he or she might say something like this to a friend, "I don't tell everybody what I am about to say, but I think I can trust you. I am kind of funny about what I eat. One of the things I just can't stand is eggplant. I'm always afraid of going to a friend's house to eat and having them serve me eggplant. That would be so embarrassing!

"I know this may sound silly to you, but I'm really sensitive about it. So please keep this confidential, because if other kids find out, I might get teased a lot about it."

After confiding something like this in a friend, your teen should talk to the people this friend talks to. If these people begin to tease your teen for not liking eggplant, then he or she has learned that the friend confided in can't be trusted; and all it cost was a little eggplant—no personally damaging information was involved.

Young people who wisely test a person's ability to keep confidences before they open up to them are less likely to be hurt then those naive enough to trust an untried friendship. In fact, a wise young person will not share any more of himself or herself with a friend than that friend is willing to invest in him or her. When friends are comfortable in confiding in each other, they may want to develop a deeper relationship.

3. BECOMING DEPENDENT UPON EACH OTHER. During this stage, friends become mutually dependent. They want to see more of each other.

These times together are not necessarily "dates." They may visit in each other's home, go to church together, meet at school during free times, and so on. They want to talk more frequently on the telephone. They become mutually dependent.

4. DOING THINGS FOR EACH OTHER. Finally, their relationship reaches the place where they begin to meet different needs for each other. For example, teens in junior-high school or high school may help each other study for exams. A young man may be good in math and a young lady may be good in English. So they might lend their expertise to each other and become not only dependent upon each other, but meet each other's needs to this extent.

When older young people are involved, the young man may take the young woman certain places in his car. She may invite him to her home for a meal.

When young people are out of high school and away from their parents' homes, a young man may fix his girl friend's car. She may invite him over for a meal, or she may do some light laundry for him.

Once your teen's relationship with a friend is through the fourth stage he or she will find that their rapport is closer and the whole cycle of stages begins to repeat itself. Lasting friendships are built through this kind of circular experience.

Be Careful in Your Choice of Friends!

Your teens' friends are helping to shape their destinies. Their friends will bring out the best or worst in them. Caution your teens to be sure their friends are deserving of what they are investing in them.

CHRIST SHOULD BE OUR CLOSEST FRIEND. Your teens need to understand how important it is for them to keep Christ as their best friend. Assure them that He will never let them down. When they experience the tragic pain of being betrayed by a friend, remind them of Christ's betrayal and urge them to seek comfort from the Lord.

Share with them times in your life when your friendship with Christ has had to provide you the courage to overcome your betrayal by your friends. Help them understand that they can always count on the Lord to be there when they need Him.

True friends are our greatest treasures. The earlier in life your teens discover this, the wiser they will be.

Eventually, through the skillful use of this friendship-building process, they will meet someone with whom they will want to spend the rest of their lives. Choosing a mate is such an important choice in life that I have devoted the whole next chapter to prepare your teens for this decision.

Ten

Mate Selection—
Chance or Choice!

---◆---

The choice of a mate is one of the most important decisions of your life. However most of us have very little training for making it.

In some cultures, the mate selection system is so far removed from the couple who are getting married it seems inhumane. In many parts of the world, parents may negotiate the marriage of their children. Places still exist where a man may buy his bride from her father.

Although, from the child's point of view, such mate selection systems seem cruel, these arranged marriages may to result in more stable families than we have in the United States. Yet we still believe our mate selection system is the right one for us, if not the best in the world; we believe this in spite of the fact that we have one of the highest divorce rates of all nations.

Perhaps our system would work better for our young people if they knew more about it and were trained in its use. After all, the more familiar a person is with our process of mate selection, the wiser he or she is likely to be in the choice of a mate.

In order to familiarize your teens with the process, you may need to get better acquainted with it yourself. So in this chapter I want to consider four important questions about our culture's approach to mate selection: When does mate selection begin? What are the stages in our mate selection process? How do people usually decide to marry? Where does the will of God fit in this process?

When Does Our Mate Selection Process Begin?

In the broadest sense, mate selection begins at birth. Believe it or not, who your parents are and where you happen to be born do place limits on your mate selection. Proximity is a factor! Your teens' mates will come from among the young people they know. After all, a person is not likely to marry someone he or she has never met.

The longer you have lived close to the person you marry, the less likely you are to be unpleasantly surprised by his or her behavior after marriage. Your teens need to know that it is risky to choose a mate from among recent acquaintances. This is one of the factors which makes college-campus courtships such a gamble.

Young people who meet in college have not had the advantages of growing up together. They don't know each other's family. When these couples marry, they are much more likely to find their families to be incompatible than are those couples who grew up together in the same church or neighborhood.

Usually a person's safest mate choice will be found among those with whom he or she has grown up. One of the important advantages of young people marrying someone from their home church is that they know each other's family. The more compatible the families of the bride and groom are, the more compatible the couple is likely to be once they are married.

ATTRACTIVENESS PLAYS AN IMPORTANT ROLE! Among those your teens will get to know are some who will be more attractive to them than others. Physical attraction tends to play too large a part in our mate selection. We cannot ignore it. However wise parents will encourage their teens to look beyond this admittedly important, but superficial, characteristic of a person.

SOCIAL BACKGROUND. Young people from similar social backgrounds tend to be more comfortable with each other. Social distance stresses marriages! Whenever young people try to bridge too great a social distance in their choice of a mate, they are subjecting their marriage to great risk. Your teens need to clearly understand this.

SIMILAR ATTITUDES AND VALUES. Of course, Christian young people are to marry someone who shares their faith.

> Be ye not unequally yoked together with unbelievers: for what fellowship hath righteousness with unrighteousness? and what communion hath light with darkness? And what concord hath Christ with Belial? or what part hath he that believeth with an infidel? And what agreement hath the temple of God with idols? for ye are the temple of the living God; as God hath said, I will dwell in them . . .; and I will be their God, and they shall be my people. Wherefore come out from among them, and be ye separate, saith the Lord, and touch not the unclean thing; and I will receive you, And will be a Father unto you, and ye shall be my sons and daughters, saith the Lord Almighty.
>
> 2 Corinthians 6:14–18

Couples who obey this biblical admonition are assured of a common core of attitudes and values around which to build their future together.

COMPLEMENTARY NEEDS. As the old saying goes, "Opposites attract." An outgoing person often chooses a mate who is more quiet and reflective. Frequently a person who takes great risks will marry someone with great needs for security.

READINESS FOR MARRIAGE. Timing plays a highly significant role in mate selection. A young person may meet someone who would make him or her a great mate. They may even be attracted to each other. However, if one or the other is not ready for marriage, they are not likely to marry.

What Are the Stages in Our Mate-Selection Process?

First, there is the *initial dating stage*. This usually occurs in junior-high school. Most young men and women find the first date an extremely awkward event. After all, we are seldom polished at anything we attempt for the first time.

Your teens will need to be reassured that times together with their boyfriends or girl friends will become more comfortable and enjoyable as they gain experience in dating.

Don't forget the important role you play in making your son's girl friends and your daughter's boyfriends feel comfortable when they are with you. Nothing is so frightening to a teen on that initial dating experience as meeting the parents of his or her date.

Why don't you take the initiative in putting them at ease? Don't overlook the extent to which this kind of thoughtfulness strengthens your own bond with your son or daughter.

Second, *random dating* begins. This is the most important stage in our mate selection process. By dating a number of partners, young men and young women begin to build a mental image of the best and worst in each of their dating partners. This mental picture becomes a valuable tool in their search for a compatible mate.

Parents should encourage their young people to continue random dating through their late teens and into their early twenties. After all, the more people your children go with, the clearer the definition they will have of the characteristics they want in an eventual mate.

The temporary nature of these relationships also helps young people more easily manage the extent of their physical involvement with each other. The more boyfriends your daughter has or the more girl friends your son has, the less likely he or she is to become the victim of an overheated relationship.

Third, young people begin to *go steady* with someone. Going steady tests the durability of the relationship. It gives a couple an opportunity to discover whether or not they can tolerate an exclusive relationship with each other over an extended period of time. If they tire of each other or cannot be true to each other during this time, they should have serious doubts about carrying their relationship any farther.

When a couple enjoys this exclusive nature of their relationship, they begin to develop deeper feelings for each other. This is a good time to begin taking a deeper look at each other's family. Later in this chapter I will be giving some specific things that young women and young men should look for in each other's family.

Fourth, a couple enters into a *preengagement understanding*. If a couple's relationship survives the closer look of going steady, they may want to enter a preengagement understanding. During this time the two of them begin to talk about marriage.

After they have explored issues of family and personal compatibility and examined their ability to manage the financial responsibilities of marriage, a couple may be ready to share with their parents the news of their intentions to marry.

Fifth, a couple becomes *engaged*. The beginning of the engagement period is marked by a young man asking his girl friend's father for the privilege of marrying her. Following parental consent, an engagement ring on the third finger of a young woman's left hand announces to the public the couple's engagement.

In seminars for singles, young women often ask me, "When can I be sure that my boyfriend seriously loves me?" I smile and say, "When he makes a sizeable investment in something he places on the third finger of your left hand. Until then, don't accuse him of being insincere when he says he loves you, but don't take him too seriously either. Remember, Jesus said that where a man's treasure was, there would his heart be also" (Matthew 6:21).

Healthy engagements seldom last less than six months or extend longer than two years. Couples who have known each other less than six months are taking a tremendous risk in marrying. They simply don't know each other well enough to marry. If a couple has been engaged for longer than two years, this extended engagement usually reflects doubts and questions the two of them need to seriously consider before they decide to go ahead with their marriage.

If strong doubts about the relationship persist, the engagement should be broken. Broken engagements are severely painful, but they don't hurt as much as broken marriages do.

Four Chances to Opt Out!

Notice, a couple who understands our mate selection system will have four opportunities for opting out of a relationship. If the chemistry and interest aren't there, a couple should never go steady. If they decide to go steady and find things in each other's family they cannot accept, they should withdraw from the relationship. After the preengagement understanding, they still have time to change their minds if one or the other battles doubts or questions he or she can't overcome. Engagement gives them one more chance to be sure about their decision to marry.

Help your young people understand that the purpose of each of these stages is not to further lock them into the relationship but rather to give them a gracious, though at times painful, way out. Young men and women who understand the built-in safeguards these gradual steps of commitment provide them are less likely to be victims of the system and are more likely to use it wisely in their search for a mate.

How Do People Decide to Marry?

At the time of the wedding, couples insist they are getting married because they love each other. In the twenty-six years I was a pastor, every couple that I married were convinced they were madly in love with each other.

A few years afterward, many can view their marriage objectively enough to see that there were powerful, less obvious influences at work in their decision to marry. Some of these influences become apparent in our culture's informal mate selection process.

The Double-Funnel Theory of Mate Selection

Young people who are not given the opportunity to learn our formal mate-selection system often become victims of our informal one. In this approach to marriage, young men are seen as primarily seeking "contact" with young women. Young women are seen as seeking "commitment" from young men.

FIVE STAGES OF PHYSICAL CONTACT. There are five clearly discernible levels of physical contact in a love relationship. The first is simply holding hands. Do you remember what a big thrill it was when you first held hands with your boyfriend or girl friend? As a young man, you feared she wouldn't let you. As a young woman, you feared he would never try.

However, as contact continues, the levels of intimacy become much more personal than holding hands. The second level of contact is what our generation called necking. That is activity above the shoulders. Then there is petting—activity above the waist; heavy petting—activity below the waist; and finally intercourse.

Soon after a couple begin to go together, the young man makes his first move for contact. If the woman grants it, she has begun her trip down the woman's funnel. However she usually requires the young man to make some commitment to her in return for the contact she permits.

He begins his trip down the man's funnel with his first commitment. However he soon wants more intimate contact, so he pressures the woman for it. If she decides to permit him more contact, then she requires more commitment from him in return.

When the young man makes a greater commitment to his young woman, he insists on more contact. If the young woman grants it, she demands more commitment in return.

As you can readily see, the farther down the funnel you go, the slipperier it gets. The next thing the couple knows they have decided to marry, and they are not quite sure at what point down the funnel they made that decision. Now do you understand why it is called the double-funnel theory of mate selection?

Marriage is too important for a couple to back into it with this kind of unconscious decision to marry. Your sons and daughters deserve a better way of making this important choice. They need to understand the serious implications of intimate levels of physical contact in their dating relationships.

Christian young people should be determined to save the deeper levels of intimacy for marriage. I have already given a biblical rationale for this advice in chapter five, "Looking Forward to Marriage," but I will summarize it again.

Saving the deeper levels of physical intimacy for marriage:

1. *Assures your teens of the ability to form the most cohesive bond possible with their future mates.*
2. *Eliminates the risk of feeling sexually "used" and rejected or feeling guilty for having sexually "used" someone else.*
3. *Eliminates the risk of pregnancy.*

Where Does the Will of God Fit In?

Although Christians choose their mates from among believers, they usually use the mate selection system of their culture in making their choices. Therefore they are subject to its risks.

Of course, God can guide a believer in his or her choice of a mate, but the believer's judgment is also involved. Otherwise, if God sovereignly chose each believer's mate, every believing couple would be ideally suited to each other. It doesn't take a very observant person to realize this is not the case.

Only rarely in the Scriptures is God found arbitrarily and providentially selecting a believer's mate. As a rule, Bible characters normally found their mates through their culture's mate-selection processes. As a result the Scriptures faithfully reveal the weaknesses of some of their marriages. Abraham and Sarah, Isaac and

Rebekah, Job and his wife, and Ananias and Sapphira all had troubled marriages.

Your Teen Must Make a Responsible Choice

If a young person is to benefit from any spiritual direction in the choice of a mate, he or she must follow New Testament priorities in this decision-making process. So, encourage your teens to consider the:

SPIRITUAL ABOVE THE MATERIAL. In His Sermon on the Mount Jesus taught, "But seek ye first the kingdom of God, and his righteousness; and all these things shall be added unto you" (Matthew 6:33).

Young people who put Christ first in their lives have a common core of values around which to build a meaningful life together. They also have the strength of their common commitment to Him to hold them together during difficult times.

UNSEEN ABOVE THE SEEN. In 2 Corinthians 4:18 Paul writes, "While we look not at the things which are seen, but at the things which are not seen: for the things which are seen are temporal; but the things which are not seen are eternal."

Encourage your teen to look for the hidden qualities in the person he or she may consider as a mate. Today's generation places such an exaggerated emphasis on physical appearance. It is important to marry someone you consider to be attractive to you; however time takes its toll on that physical attraction. A person's character is what you are left to live with.

Encourage your teens to look for honesty, loyalty, courage, dependability, responsibility, fairness, kindness, ambition, and love. These are qualities that will be enhanced by time.

The Family Is Important

The Bible places great importance on the choice of the family as well as the mate. So let me suggest some things you might tell your daughter to look for in a young man's father when she is seriously considering the young man as a potential mate.

Notice how the young man's father treats his mother. After all, this is the way that young man has been taught to treat women. Does his father show his mother affection and tenderness? Does he compliment her? Is he kind to her? Does he put her before the children in his attention? How does he relate to his daughters, the young man's sisters, if he has any?

The way the young man's father relates to the females of the family should be seen as a strong influence on the way the young man will relate to your daughter, if they should marry.

Here are some things your son should notice about the mother of a girl he is thinking of as a potential mate. Does the girl's mother have a discernible figure? If she is still concerned about her weight and physical appearance, she probably is still very much in love with her husband. Does she still flirt with her husband? Does she seem to enjoy being a wife more than she enjoys being a mother?

The way the young woman's mother relates to her father is going to be a strong influence on how this young lady relates to her future husband.

Emphasize the importance of marrying into a strong and healthy Christian family. This is particularly important if your own marriage has been broken by divorce.

Your children may think this is putting too much emphasis on the family. They may object, "But I'm not marrying the family!" Tell them how wrong they are about this. Help them to see that when they marry the son or daughter, they are marrying the whole family. Warn them that it is a serious mistake to marry a young man or young woman if they don't like his or her family.

Premarital Counseling Is a Must!

Competent premarital counseling is marriage insurance your son or daughter cannot afford to go without. After all, marriage is a task to be accomplished. A person who doesn't have adequate information about the task or competent skills for accomplishing it is not likely to succeed in it. A good premarital counseling program will address both of these needs.

You will never take all the risk out of mate selection for your children. However if you provide your teens with the practical helps presented in this chapter, they are going to be better prepared for making a wise choice than many of their peers.

Part V

Helping Your Teens Develop Their Faith

Eleven

Helping Your Teens Define Their Values

Between the ages of twelve and twenty-five, most of us make the three biggest decisions of our lives: our values, our vocations, and our mates. The most important of these is our values.

Although the church can assist in value education, most of our values are learned in the home.

The importance of values to a young person's mental and spiritual health is widely accepted. Here is what the Joint Commission on the Mental Health of Children has said on the subject:

> It is recognized today that a positive set of values by which a person may live is not alone a subject of concern to philosophers and theologians, it also is very much a sickness and health issue for the individual.
>
> In the past three decades, modern psychology and psychiatry have demonstrated that people who are unable to cultivate values which deepen their sense of security, be-

longing, and self acceptance often find themselves over-whelmed by the psychologically incapacitating effects of sickness or the many other forms of stress with which they are confronted.[12]

Helping your teens discover and define the values of their faith will make an invaluable contribution to the total health and productivity of their lives.

In assisting you with this task, I want to explore the following questions: What are values? When are values formed? Why should parents be concerned about their teens' values? How can you help your teens clarify their values?

Ethics, the science of behavior, helps us differentiate among values, attitudes, tastes, and fads—four distinguishable reflections of a person's culture. Two important dimensions in which these cultural expressions differ are *importance* and *durability*. When these differences are displayed on a continuum, they are readily recognized.

Differences Among Four Cultural Espressions

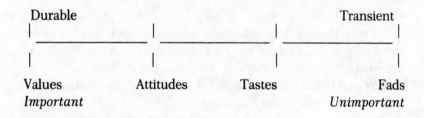

What Are Values?

Values are ideals that give meaning to our existence. These are the most deeply held and durable expressions of a person's beliefs. The more clearly a person's values are defined, the more ethically predictable that person's behavior is likely to be.

Honesty, responsibility, courtesy, loyalty, fairness, excellence, charity, orderliness, cleanliness, justice, freedom, honor—these are examples of values most American parents would want their children to embrace.

What Are Attitudes?

Attitudes are emotionally toned predispositions to react in a predictable manner, favorable or unfavorable, toward persons, objects, or ideas. They are not as deeply held or long lasting as values, but attitudes still play a powerful role in determining our behavior. Here are some examples.

The word *devil* provokes a negative response almost everywhere. Most Christians also will react negatively to the name of *Judas*. On the other hand, people in the Western world are likely to respond favorably to the names of *Moses* and *Jesus*.

The Bible and the American flag are objects responded to favorably in our society. On the other hand, jails and guns are more likely to provoke a negative response.

The idea of communism is rejected by Americans, but the idea of competition will be embraced by most of us.

Our reactions to these persons, objects, and ideas are predictable. We have definite attitudes toward them.

What Are Tastes?

Tastes are aesthetic preferences or likings. They are less durable among our beliefs than either values or attitudes. Nevertheless, during the time we embrace them, they do affect our behavior in predictable ways. If you know a person's tastes, you can predict his or her choices in given situations.

Our tastes are reflected in our choices of food, drinks, colors, cars, clothes, hairstyles, fragrances, music, and so on.

What Are Fads?

Fads are temporary trends that for a time are followed with exaggerated zeal. These are the most transient of our cultural manifestation. However they add interest and momentary excitement to our lives.

Hula-hoops, yo-yos, white tennis shoes, designer jeans, and Rubic cubes are examples of fads that have come and gone among us during the last three decades. No one would contend that any of these are deep parts of America, but during their brief stay among us, they added color to our lives.

As you can see, although each of these (values, attitudes, tastes, and fads) is a part of our culture, they vary greatly in permanence and importance. For example some things about being American are more deeply ingrained in our culture than others.

Understanding the relative nature of some of our native cultural expressions will help your teens begin to sort out the relative importance of some of the aspects of their faith and philosophy of life. Young people need to discover that everything they believe is not of equal importance. Their values are more deeply ingrained in their characters and have a more durable influence upon their lives than their attitudes, tastes, or fads.

When Are Values Formed?

Values are learned gradually during childhood and adolescence, mainly through subtle family communication. As you know, parental modeling is the primary method of communicating values.

Parents Are the Teachers of Values

As young people mature intellectually they need a more rational understanding of their spiritual and moral values than can be gained by simply imitating their parents. Peter underscores the importance of being able to give reasons for your hope. In 1 Peter 3:15 he says, ". . . And be ready always to give an answer to every man that asketh you a reason of the hope that is in you. . . ." With you lie the responsibility and the opportunity to help your teens discover practical answers for those who inquire about their faith.

Home Is the School Where Values Are Learned

Remember, the home is the environment in which spiritual values are taught and learned. Your teens will gain their basic impressions of what it means to be a Christian from their home. Many parents mistakenly expect the institutional church to perform this task for them, but this is impossible. At best, the church can only reinforce the values of the home. If Christian values are not taught in the home, it is highly unlikely that the church or the Christian school will be able to compensate for this deficiency in your youngsters' moral education. So take advantage of the moments you have with your teenagers to answer their questions and challenge them to think through the issues of their faith.

How Morally Mature Are Your Teens?

Discover why your teens choose right over wrong. To test the level of their moral maturity, you might ask, "Why do drivers stop at traffic lights?"

Here are some typical answers you might anticipate. "To keep from getting a traffic ticket for going through a red light." "To avoid an accident." "To obey the law." "To allow everyone a fair opportunity to use the intersection safely."

Of course, as you can see, each answer to the question reflects a slightly higher level of moral judgment than the answer preceding it. On which of the following four levels of moral judgment do your teens appear to be functioning?

FEAR OF PUNISHMENT. Do they choose right over wrong because of a fear of punishment? The only goodness a punishment-oriented morality produces comes from the fear of being bad.

Young people who operate from this basis do not understand the benefits of doing what is right. They only know the pain of not doing what is right. Therefore when they do the right thing, they are unable to explain why it is right. They are simply trying to avoid the pain of not doing it.

DESIRE FOR PLEASURE. When young people do what is right because it also happens to be what is pleasurable, their actions are not prompted by the moral obligation to do what is right. They are simply choosing to do the most pleasurable thing at the time.

GROUP EXPECTATIONS. Sometimes young people determine what is right from the expectations of the group they happen to be with at the time. If they were with a group who had different expectations, they would conform to those. Their actions are not really governed by their own morality, but by the expectations of the group. Pleasing their peers determines what is right for them.

RESPECT FOR UNIVERSAL MORAL LAW. If your teens are to function on this level of morality, you will need to explain God's moral laws to them and help them understand why it is in their best interests to respect these. This is the kind of quality communication around matters of faith that produces moral convictions in your teens.

Why Should Parents Be Concerned?

In middle adolescence, your teens are capable of deductive and systematic thinking for the first time in their lives. They are experiencing a birth of idealism—the difference between the world as it is and the world as it ought to be is becoming apparent to them.

The distance observed between these two worlds creates tremendous tensions within young people. Often these tensions play a critical role in triggering off rebellion or religious conversions.

At the same time, teens are developing a sense of history that enables them to compare the present with the distant past and the future. With a little help, they are able to anticipate the long-range moral implications of various plans of action they may have.

This is the time when they are most likely to examine your values closely. No doubt they will criticize some of them and question others. However, if they see your life as one that brings you satisfaction and fulfillment, they are unlikely to completely turn aside from it to embrace an untried path for their futures.

This examination of your values makes it so important for you to seek opportunities to share your Christian faith with them—not simply in an evangelistic way, but in a philosophical way. Help them understand the practicality of your faith and the personal rewards you have reaped from it. Present Christianity as not only a way to heaven, but also a way to live on earth—a culture of its own—with its own set of values, attitudes, tastes, and fads.

The Christian Life Is a Culture

As a culture not every aspect of the Christian faith is of equal importance. Remember, Jesus chided the religious people of His day for not knowing the difference between the gnats and camels or motes and beams of their faith.

Young people need to know how to differentiate the more important matters of their faith from those of lesser importance. Perhaps the easiest way for you to help them discern these is to familiarize them with the Christian faith in ethical terms—teaching them to identify its values, attitudes, tastes, and fads.

Kingdom Values

Remember, *values* are ideals that give meaning to our existence. They are the most durable parts of a culture. You cannot compromise your values and maintain your culture.

Kingdom values are central to the meaning of the Christian faith. To compromise them is to betray your faith.

What are some biblical truths that are this vital to an expression of the kingdom? Without attempting to give an exhaustive list, let me suggest some.

1. THE ATONEMENT. Paul succinctly defines the atonement in Romans 5:8–11:

> But God commendeth his love toward us, in that, while we were yet sinners, Christ died for us. Much more then, being now justified by his blood, we shall be saved from wrath through him. For if, when we were enemies, we were reconciled to God by the death of his Son; much more, being reconciled, we shall be saved by his life. And not only so, but we also joy in God through our Lord Jesus Christ, by whom we have received the atonement.

Christ's substitutionary death for sin is the basis for fallen humanity's relationship with God. Jesus, in His incarnation, crucifixion, burial, resurrection, and ascension will continue to be as central to the church's identity in eternity as He is today. Therefore, the atonement qualifies as a basic value of evangelical Christianity.

2. THE BEATITUDES. Jesus begins his Sermon on the Mount with the beatitudes (Matthew 5:3–12):

> Blessed are the poor in spirit: for theirs is the kingdom of heaven.
> Blessed are they that mourn: for they shall be comforted.
> Blessed are the meek: for they shall inherit the earth.
> Blessed are they which do hunger and thirst after righteousness: for they shall be filled.
> Blessed are the merciful: for they shall obtain mercy.
> Blessed are the pure in heart: for they shall see God.
> Blessed are the peacemakers: for they shall be called the children of God.
> Blessed are they which are persecuted for righteousness' sake: for theirs is the kingdom of heaven.
> Blessed are ye, when men shall revile you, and persecute you, and shall say all manner of evil against you falsely, for my sake. Rejoice, and be exceeding glad: for great is your reward in heaven: for so persecuted they the prophets which were before you.

These principles are at the very heart of kingdom living. Now we can only approximate them, even with God's grace in our lives. However in eternity they will be the governing attributes of kingdom living.

3. THE COMMANDMENTS. Given to Moses by God on Mount Sinai, the ten commandments have been the heart of the Judeo-Christian ethic. The commandments are listed in Exodus 20:1–17 and Deuteronomy 5:6–21.

1. *Thou shalt have no other gods before me.*
2. *Thou shalt not make unto thee any graven image.*
3. *Thou shalt not take the name of the Lord thy God in vain.*
4. *Remember the sabbath day, to keep it holy.*
5. *Honour thy father and thy mother: that thy days may be long upon the land which the Lord thy God giveth thee.*
6. *Thou shalt not kill.*
7. *Thou shalt not commit adultery.*
8. *Thou shalt not steal.*
9. *Thou shalt not bear false witness against thy neighbour.*
10. *Thou shalt not covet.*

Young people should understand that these are not rules in the legalistic sense of the word. They are moral laws—universal principles. The commandments govern our relationships to God, our mates, our parents, our children, and our neighbors. When we live by these principles, we reap their rewards. When we don't, we suffer the consequences.

4. DISCIPLES' PRAYER. In Matthew 6:9–13, Jesus taught His disciples to pray:

. . . Our Father which art in heaven, Hallowed be thy name. Thy kingdom come. Thy will be done in earth, as it is in heaven. Give us this day our daily bread. And forgive us our debts, as we forgive our debtors. And lead us not into temptation, but deliver us from evil: For thine is the kingdom, and the power, and the glory, for ever. Amen.

This prayer expresses the priorities of Christian living. God's will and the coming of His kingdom to earth are uppermost in the Christian's concerns. After these come the material concerns of earning a living, forgiving and being forgiven, and victory in our struggle with evil. Maintaining these priorities is the heart of spiritual discipline.

5. THE ETERNAL WORD. The evangelical Christian is identified with an uncompromising defense of Scripture as the inerrant Word of God. Paul declares, "All scripture is given by inspiration of God, and is profitable for doctrine, for reproof, for correction, for instruction in righteousness: That the man of God may be perfect, thoroughly furnished unto all good works" (2 Timothy 3:16, 17).

Although allowance is made for different translations and interpretations of Scripture, the evangelical Christian believes that as the Word of God was transmitted in the original languages, authors were protected from erring through divine inspiration. As Peter states, "Knowing this first, that no prophecy of the scripture is of any private interpretation. For the prophecy came not in old time by the will of man: but holy men of God spake as they were moved by the Holy Ghost" (2 Peter 1:20, 21).

Kingdom Attitudes

Although attitudes are not as central to the meaning of a culture as are values, they do play an important role in defining various subcultures within a larger culture. For example, Americans share a common core of values that identify us as a people. However, among us are those with conflicting attitudes toward various aspects of our public life who are known as Democrats and Republicans. Both groups are Americans—they share a common core of values. However they differ in their ideas as to how those values can best be expressed.

Among Christians there are various denominations. Although all evangelicals share a common set of Christian values, we find definite differences over various expressions of the Christian faith such as the mode and time of water baptism, the frequency and method of celebrating communion, and the security of the believer. Denominations are identified by the positions they take in these areas of difference.

Explain your denominational position to your teens. Give them the biblical reasons that support it. This will help them respect their church more. However encourage them to take a charitable and tolerant view toward others who may differ. After all, our common identity as Christians is more important to the kingdom of God than our denominational differences.

Kingdom Tastes

Kingdom tastes are even more peripheral to our identity as Christians than denominations. They have more to do with style of worship and musical preferences.

Some Christians feel more comfortable with a liturgical form of worship. The organization and structure make it easier for them to meaningfully participate in worship. On the other hand, other Christians find liturgical worship too formal and impersonal. They prefer a more spontaneous approach.

In similar ways, the musical preferences of Christians differ. Some prefer more traditional organ and choral music. They find the historical roots of this music give depth to their Christian identity. Others prefer the gospel songs of the twentieth century as the musical expression of their faith. They like the evangelistic emphasis and intimate personal dimension of this music. Still others prefer the emphasis contemporary gospel music places on the immediate in spiritual experience.

While teaching your teens to worship comfortably in your church, help them to develop an appreciation for other styles of worship as well. Expose them to a variety of Christian musical expressions. Respect their preferences, and teach them to respect yours. Such breadth of tastes will allow your teens to be comfortable with a broad segment of the Christian community.

Kingdom Fads

Remember, fads are temporary trends that for a time are followed with exaggerated zeal. In Christianity these might be such transient interests as methods of evangelism or some unique expression of spiritual experience.

Fads add color to a culture, but they aren't to be mistaken for values. Realizing this will help your teens avoid embracing fads too tenaciously or resisting them too heatedly.

While you engage your teens in the kinds of conversations designed to help them clarify their values, you will be sharpening up your own. After all, one of the best ways to learn is to teach.

Religious Values Are Unique!

The Joint Commission on the Mental Health of Children challenges parents to help their youngsters develop healthy spiritual values.

> While many aspects of society project values—social, economic, cultural—which the individual can utilize to achieve positive emotional status, those values derived from religious sources have something distinctive and timeless to offer which supplement the values society provides.
>
> Such distinction as the affirmation of the infinite worth of the individual, the capacity to face the ultimate questions of life with equanimity, and the acceptance of man's reason for being are an indication of the kind of uniqueness religion offers.

No other aspect of parenthood is more important than the moral preparation of your children for life. No other institution is more directly involved in this critical task than the home. No other people are more important to the mission than you—their parents.

In the next chapter, I will be presenting a developmental model for helping you teach your teens to separate the magical and the superstitious from the supernatural.

Twelve

Maturing in Faith

———◆———

Somewhere between your youngsters' eleventh and thirteenth years, a giant leap toward mental maturity takes place. By the time they reach mental age fifteen, their abstracting ability is at its peak. From that time on, they have the mental equipment to talk to you about any subject you care to share with them.

Ideally, dialogue about your faith with your children never ceases. It begins when they are old enough to understand the simplest truth and continues right on through adolescence into adulthood. This type of communication was the primary method of religious education for Jewish children in Bible times. In Deuteronomy 6:4–7 Moses says:

> Hear, O Israel: the Lord our God is one Lord: And thou shalt love the Lord thy God with all thine heart, and with all thy soul, and with all thy might. And these words, which I

command thee this day, shall be in thine heart: And thou shalt teach them diligently unto thy children, and shalt talk of them when thou sittest in thine house, and when thou walkest by the way, and when thou liest down, and when thou risest up.

Talking informally with your children about matters of faith is an excellent method of religious instruction. Many young people are going to resist any effort you make toward formal Bible study. Some of us who have unpleasant memories about family altars can understand their resistance.

Keep Family Devotions Brief!

My grandmother was a dedicated Christian, but she didn't know much about teaching children to value spiritual things. When she was in our home, she led our family altar. She conducted it for adults—not for children or teens. We all had to kneel. The adults prayed first. My grandmother had a great burden for missions. She prayed for every nation God laid on her heart. She prayed for each member of our family. When she finished, the other adults took their turns.

Of course, before the first adult was done praying, we children were pinching and poking at each other—and we were punished for this misbehavior.

So you can see why children prefer very brief informal periods of family devotions, and these are adequate to maintain spiritual discipline in your family. However even more valuable times of instruction are those informal moments of dialogue with your children about the things of God.

The remainder of this chapter will be devoted to providing you with some guidelines to follow and some subjects to discuss as you help your children mature in faith.

Give Teens Reasons for Rules

Teens need rules, but they find it frustrating to be restricted without understanding why. Even when they don't have the courage to face you with their complaints, they are mumbling protests to themselves. "Why won't my parents let me smoke?" "Why won't my parents let me drink?" "Why must I be in by eleven?" "Why can't I dance?"

Young people deserve a logical explanation for the parental morality they are expected to observe. They may not want to accept your explanation, but you owe it to them anyway.

RULES WITHOUT REASONS PROVOKE REBELLION. If you can't defend your rules with some sound reasons, then you'd better question their wisdom. If you have sound reasons for them, explain these to your teens. This communication will help them to respect your rules, even if they don't agree with them.

When you require your teens to keep rules you don't explain, you invite rebellion. Some parents complain, "We never questioned our parents' rules, and we never rebelled. So why should our kids question our rules?"

Even though this may have been the case, most of us would admit that our faith would have been more practical and our morality healthier, if our parents had given us a sound explanation for their rules. Parents should think twice about trying to enforce rules they can't explain.

DICE—OR A SPINNER! Years ago I knew of some parents who were so opposed to gambling and so fearful of it that they wouldn't allow their children to play any game that involved rolling dice. So when their children were asked to play Monopoly with friends, they couldn't play because players are required to roll dice to indicate the number of spaces they move ahead on the board. Their friends would use a spinner from another game to determine their moves so these friends would be able to play.

Of course they resented not being able to play the game like other children. The fact that their parents never explained why they were not permitted to use dice in playing Monopoly only intensified their resentment. Such a rule made them feel odd and peculiar among their friends—and to make matters worse, they didn't know the reason for it.

Their parents never did explain to them that gambling had been a real financial threat to their home and marriage. They never gave them reasons for any of the other rules they imposed on them either. Because they didn't know the reasons for their rules, they didn't respect their morality.

Most parents have good sound moral reasons for their rules. If you haven't defined the moral reasons for your rules—do that! Then communicate these reasons to your children.

For example, I know you don't want your children to smoke—and you have good reasons for this. Smoking damages the body. On every package of cigarettes the surgeon general requires a health warning to be posted.

Therefore, in placing tobacco off limits for your children, explain to them, "I don't want you to smoke because smoking harms our bodies. People who smoke are more likely to get cancer of the lungs and have heart problems than are people who don't smoke."

MORE SUBTLE RISKS. What about something like dancing? Many parents who disapprove of dancing for teens believe the motions and rhythms involved excite sexual passions and increase sexual risks. If you don't want your teenagers to dance because you are concerned about these risks, tell them.

However, be sure they understand that dancing can be an enjoyable activity for a married couple in the privacy of their home. When parents assume a strict legalistic stance against dancing without bothering to give young people any explanation for this restriction, young people often assume that dancing would be evil under any circumstances—even for a married couple.

SEX AND VIOLENCE. Be sure your teens understand why fantasy material that involves illicit sex or graphic violence is unhealthy and destructive. Point out the brutal and dehumanizing dimensions of pornography. Expose the unrealistic expectations it fosters. After all, young people have enough difficulty controlling the normal sexual and aggressive urges they feel without having those urges overstimulated by inappropriate fantasy material.

While opposing pornography, encourage your teens to anticipate what married love will be like. Let them know that sexual fantasies are normal and healthy, so long as they are related to marriage. Encourage your high-school teens to read the Song of Solomon and discuss it with them. Be sure that they know they have your blessing in dreaming of the day when their sexual fantasies will be fulfilled in a Christian marriage.

CURFEWS. With rare exceptions, junior-high girls should be home by 11:00 P.M. and senior-high students by midnight. Young men will usually need an extra half hour for taking their girl friends home. College students who are living at home should be in by 1:00 A.M. After all, in most communities there are very few constructive activities that occur after midnight.

That's why parents who love their children insist on reasonable curfews. Your teens know these curfews are fair, so don't take their protests too seriously.

Teens may choose to rebel against some of these restrictions; but if you have explained the principles underlying your rules, they will know what they are rebelling against—and they will have a clear understanding of the risks they are taking.

Religious Experience Should Promote Growth

More religious conversions occur between fifteen and seventeen years of age than at any other similar period throughout the life span. This is partly due to the tension created between the teen's ideals and the realities of his or her life. Religious conversion is one of the ways youngsters find for resolving these tensions. However, if their religious experience is going to be healthy, it must provide for their growth.

When I was going to college, I was somewhat anxious about the potential conflict between my spiritual experience and my academic pursuits. During that time, the Holy Spirit helped me coin the following phrase, which served to balance these two very important dimensions of my life.

To live is to grow; to grow is to change. If we cannot discern the difference between the change that results from growth and the change that results from the loss of our faith, our fear of losing our faith can make us resist all change, so that our faith becomes an inhibitor, rather than a facilitator, of our growth.

God never wants your teens' faith to get in the way of their growth. In fact, healthy religious experiences will always be supportive of their growth.

A Developmental Model of Faith

Help your teens understand that they will grow and develop spiritually in much the same way they have grown and developed physically and emotionally.

In talking to Nicodemus, Jesus used this kind of developmental model to explain spiritual life to him. He likened spiritual birth to physical birth. Here's how John records their conversation:

There was a man of the Pharisees, named Nicodemus, a ruler of the Jews: The same came to Jesus by night, and said unto him, Rabbi, we know that thou art a teacher come from God: for no man can do these miracles that thou doest, except God be with him. Jesus answered and said unto him, Verily, Verily, I say unto thee, Except a man be born again, he cannot see the kingdom of God. Nicodemus saith unto him, How can a man be born when he is old? can he enter the second time into his mother's womb, and be born? Jesus answered, Verily, verily I say unto thee, Except a man be born of water and of the Spirit, he cannot enter into the kingdom of God. That which is born of the flesh is flesh; and that which is born of the Spirit is spirit. Marvel not that I said unto thee, Ye must be born again.

John 3:1–7

Peter uses this same model in explaining to his readers how they can grow spiritually. In 1 Peter 2:2 he says, "As newborn babes, desire the sincere milk of the word, that ye may grow thereby."

Notice how Paul uses a developmental model to emphasize the need for spiritual maturity to his Ephesian readers in order to protect them from unscrupulous teachers:

> That we henceforth be no more children, tossed to and fro, and carried about with every wind of doctrine, by the sleight of men, and cunning craftiness, whereby they lie in wait to deceive; But speaking the truth in love, may grow up into him in all things, which is the head, even Christ: From whom the whole body fitly joined together and compacted by that which every joint supplieth, according to the effectual working in the measure of every part, maketh increase of the body unto the edifying of itself in love.
>
> Ephesians 4:14–16

The acceptance of an analogous relationship between natural growth and development and spiritual growth and development on the part of the New Testament writers is further attested to by Paul's statement in 1 Corinthians 13:11, "When I was a child, I spake as a child, I understood as a child, I thought as a child: but when I became a man, I put away childish things."

In the process of developing the capacity to view the world abstractly, your children grow through a magical and superstitious way of viewing life. In much the same way, Christians often view their faith magically or superstitiously, before coming to a more mature understanding of the supernatural nature of their relationship with God.

The Magical World of the Infant

Until babies are approximately eight months old, they see their parents as having the power to make things appear and disappear at will. This magical view of parents results from the infants' inability to understand that things that are out of sight continue to exist.

For example, when a youngster six months old watches Mother put a dish in the cupboard and close the door, a look of wonder comes across his or her face, since a baby of this age is not yet capable of knowing that the dish continues to exist behind the door. From the baby's perspective, Mother has just made the dish disappear. Therefore Mother has magical power!

As Mother puts clothes in drawers and coats and sweepers in closets, this assumption of the baby is reinforced. From the baby's perspective, Dad's magical powers are even greater than Mother's since he makes bigger things, like cars and lawn mowers disappear.

So the infant believes that Mom and Dad can make anything happen. Since loving parents provide for their babies, it is easy to understand how babies could assume that Mom and Dad have no other reason to exist but to meet their needs.

Therefore, in the mind of babies, parents can easily become magical agents who exist to bring them anything they may want at the moment. The baby's cry or obvious look of displeasure is the vehicle the child uses to command this magic. When wise parents are at times unwilling to comply with this magical expectancy, temper tantrums are often displayed.

SPIRITUAL INFANTS. Many baby Christians are magical in their faith. They are so self-centered as to believe that their heavenly Father exists to do whatever they ask Him to do, provided they ask Him in the name of Jesus. "After all," they insist, "doesn't John fourteen, verses twelve through fourteen say that is the way prayer works?":

> Verily, verily, I say unto you, He that believeth on me, the works that I do shall he do also; and greater works than these shall he do; because I go unto my Father. And whatsoever ye shall ask in my name, that will I do, that the Father may be glorified in the Son. If ye shall ask any thing in my name, I will do it.

So in prayer, they present to God a list of the things they want Him to do, and they close their prayer in Jesus' name. Now from the spiritual infant's point of view, God must do everything included in the prayer, because all these things have been asked in Jesus' name. This is a perfectly normal, healthy state of faith for a spiritual infant.

However your teenagers are capable of seeing that parents have other reasons to exist than simply to do what their babies want them to do. Use that analogy to help them understand that God dearly loves His children, but He doesn't exist to do what they want Him to do.

If it were possible for us to divert His reason for being to serve our selfish ends, what would happen to the universe? On the other hand, if we can be challenged to discover His will for our lives and make it our own, the horizons of our lives will be broadened beyond our most ambitious dreams.

The Superstitious World of the Young Child

Babies grow out of their magical world view and begin to see their parents in a slightly less distorted way. Mom and Dad are still very powerful beings in their world. However, the young child now attempts to manipulate parental power by wishing and through rituals.

A child's tendency toward this kind of superstitious thinking is what feeds his or her fascination with fairy tales. Children wish for so many things that enough of them happen to reinforce their belief in the power of wishing. Consequently when they, in moments of anger, impulsively wish for something destructive to happen, they find themselves in need of a way to break the spell of the wish. This is the age when rituals for undoing destructive wishes are developed—crossing the fingers, crossing the heart, and so on.

For example, when I was a child, children would try to walk all the way to the store without stepping on a crack in the sidewalk. The superstitious jingle we would repeat to justify this exercise was, "If you step on a crack, you'll break your mother's back."

Of course, if someone shoved us or we lost our balance and stepped on a crack, then we would undo the "hex" by stepping on a crack with each step on the way back from the store.

SPIRITUAL CHILDREN. There is a childhood phase of spiritual development in which believers form strong attachments to faith "rituals" and formulas for praying. A passage of Scripture that is often misused during this time is Matthew 18:19, where Jesus says, "Again I say unto you, That if two of you shall agree on earth as touching any thing that they shall ask, it shall be done for them of my Father which is in heaven."

A spiritual child believes that all a person has to do to get anything he wants from God is to get another Christian to agree with him in prayer about it. When the two of them agree that God should grant this wish, then God must perform it—regardless of what it is. This is a superstitious approach to prayer that is normal through a person's spiritual childhood, but it is not characteristic of a mature believer's approach to prayer.

A Mature Approach to Prayer

As an evangelical Christian I believe the Bible to be infallible. Therefore, I believe Jesus was giving Christians instructions on prayer in John 14:12–14. However, I do not believe he intended this beautiful passage on prayer to be subjected to a magical interpretation that obligates God to do anything a spiritual infant requests in the name of Jesus.

Remind your teen that the present ministry of Jesus is one of prayer. He is our High Priest, our Advocate with the Father (Hebrews 4:14; 1 John 2:1). Presently He is interceding for us (Hebrews 7:25).

Mature believers are more concerned with prayer as a means of accomplishing God's will than as a way to persuade God to do their bidding. They are interested in discovering those things for which Jesus Himself is praying.

As the Holy Spirit reveals those matters on Christ's heart mature Christians begin to make those issues the focus of their prayer life.

Their prayers begin to sound more and more like Christ's prayers. They are praying less and less for the selfish things of their magical and superstitious worlds and more and more for the things God wants done in His world.

The prayer of mature believers is less magical and less superstitious, but it is still anchored in their belief in a supernatural spiritual reality. However the purpose of that reality is the accomplishment of God's will—not ours!

By allowing the Holy Spirit to lay the concerns of Christ upon our hearts, we learn to pray as though we were praying in Jesus' place. That is what praying in the name of Jesus means.

What about that passage in Matthew 18:19? The mature Christian knows that Christ is not teaching His followers a clever way for two of them to collaborate so they can manipulate God to accomplish their own selfish ends.

The key to understanding this passage is in the Greek word translated "agree." This is the same Greek word from which we get our English word *symphony*.

Obviously Jesus was teaching His disciples to trust the ability of the Holy Spirit to harmonize the prayer life of the church. That is, He was encouraging them to believe that those urgent prayer needs of the kingdom will be supernaturally communicated to believers by the Holy Spirit. He will bring two or more members of the body of Christ into agreement for these needs without any selfish collaboration on their parts. Then when two or three people meet at church and discover that the Holy Spirit is orchestrating the prayer lives of God's people by laying certain common needs on their hearts, they can be assured of these things happening.

Your middle teens can begin to understand some of these things. As they spiritually mature they can understand that the supernatural is neither magical nor superstitious. They will discover the supernatural to be simply God at work in His world, doing His will at levels of understanding beyond our comprehension. Isaiah made that discovery centuries ago. He wrote, "For my thoughts are not your thoughts, neither are your ways my ways, saith the Lord. For as the heavens are higher than the earth, so are my ways higher than your ways, and my thoughts than your thoughts" (Isaiah 55:8, 9).

By helping your teens sort out some of these apparent inconsistencies and contradictions for themselves, you will spare them many disappointments in their faith.

* * *

Throughout this book, I've had the opportunity to talk to you about some of the most valuable people in the world: your teens. My wife and I have raised three youngsters; we know there are no simple formulas for wisely managing teenagers. We know that there are exceptions to every rule, but we know that God's Word is faithful and God's grace is sufficient. He will help you be the parent you need to be and your teenagers to realize the potential God knows they can achieve in Jesus.

Source Notes

Chapter 1

1. Leonard H. Gross, ed., *The Parent's Guide to Teenagers* (New York: Macmillan Pub. Co., 1981), 253–254.
2. Benjamin B. Wolman, ed., *Handbook of Developmental Psychology* (Englewood Cliffs, N. J.: Prentice-Hall, 1982), 421–423.

Chapter 2

3. K. W. Burkhart, *Growing Into Love* (New York: G. P. Putnam, 1981), 25, 26.
4. Ibid., pp. 55, 103.

Chapter 4

5. R. B. Millman, "Drug and Alcohol Abuse," eds. B. Wallman, J. Egan, A. O. Ross, *Book of Treatment of Mental Disorders in Children and Adolescents* (Englewood Cliffs, N. J.: Prentice-Hall, 1978), 238.
6. R. E. Botvan and J. R. Acocella, *Abnormal Psychology* (New York: Random House, 1984), 291.
7. Ibid., p. 294.
8. G. G. Forest, *How to Cope With the Teenage Drinker* (New York: Atheneum, 1983), 100.

Chapter 5

9. M. S. Calderone and E. W. Johnson, *The Family Book About Sexuality* (New York: Harper & Row, 1981), 180.
10. K. W. Burkhart, *Growing Into Love* (New York: G. P. Putnam, 1981), 25.
11. Calderone and Johnson, *The Family Book*, 27.

Chapter 11

12. *Mental Health From Infancy Through Adolescence* (New York: Harper & Row, 1973), 444.

Bibliography

Abelson, H. I. et al. *National Survey on Drug Abuse: Main Findings: 1977.* Rockville, Md.: National Institute on Drug Abuse, 1977.

Bootzin, R. R. and J. R. Acocella. *Abnormal Psychology.* 4th ed. New York: Random House, 1984.

Burkhart, K. W. *Growing Into Love.* New York: G. P. Putnam, 1981.

Calderone, M. S. and E. W. Johnson. *The Family Book About Sexuality.* New York: Harper & Row, 1981.

Chumlea, W. C. "Physical Growth in Adolescence." In B. Wolman and G. Sticker, eds. *Handbook of Developmental Psychology*. Englewood Cliffs, N. J.: Prentice-Hall, 1982, 471–485.

Dreyer, P. H. "Sexuality During Adolescence." In B. Wolman and G. Stricker, eds. *Handbook of Developmental Psychology*. Englewood Cliffs, N. J.: Prentice-Hall, 1982, 559–601.

Fishburne, P. M. et al. *National Survey on Drug Abuse: Main Findings: 1979*. Rockville, Md.: National Institute on Drug Abuse, 1979.

Forrest, G. G. *How to Cope With a Teenage Drinker*. New York: Atheneum, 1983.

Gross, L. H., ed. *The Parent's Guide to Teenagers*. New York: Macmillan Pub. Co., 1981.

Hofmann, F. G. *A Handbook on Drug and Alcohol Abuse*. 2nd ed. New York: Oxford University Press, 1983.

Hopkins, J. R. *Adolescence: The Transitional Years*. New York: Academic Press, Inc., 1983.

Isralowitz, R. and M. Singer, eds. *Adolescent Substance Abuse*. Child and Youth Services, 6, New York: Haworth Press, 1983.

Joint Commission on Mental Health of Children. *Mental Health: From Infancy Through Adolescence*. New York: Harper & Row, 1973.

Leman, Kevin. *Smart Girls Don't and Guys Don't Either*. Ventura, Calif.: Regal Books, 1982.

McCary, J. L. *Human Sexuality*. Princeton, N. J.: D. Van Nostrand Co., Inc., 1967.

Miller, J. D. et al. *National Survey on Drug Abuse: Main Findings: 1982*. Rockville, Md.: National Institute on Drug Abuse, 1982.

Millman, R. B. "Drug and Alcohol Abuse." In B. Wolman, J. Egan, and A. O. Ross, eds. *Handbook of Treatment of Mental Disorders in Childhood and Adolescence*. Englewood Cliffs, N. J.: Prentice-Hall, 1978.

Otteson, O., and J. Townsend. *Kids and Drugs: A Parent's Guide*. New York: CFS Pub. Corp., 1983.

Rosenbaum, J. and V. Rosenbaum. *Living With Teenagers*. Briarcliff Manor, N. Y.: Stein & Day, 1980.

Shepherd-Look, D. L. "Sex Differentiation and the Development of Sex Roles." In B. Wolman, and G. Stricker, eds. *Handbook of Developmental Psychology*. Englewood Cliffs, N. J.: Prenctice-Hall, 1982, 403–433.

Sorensen, R. C. *Adolescent Sexuality in Contemporary America*. New York: World Publishing, 1973.